# Choosing Peace
# Through Daily Practices

# Introduction

## Peacebuilding in Violent Times

### *Ellen Ott Marshall*

As Albert Camus commented of his own time in 1957, we too are "living in an interesting era."[1] In the throes of war, horrified by the threat and reality of terrorism, our nation is grappling with vulnerability in a classic though unfortunate way. We deny the real depth of our vulnerability and the ways in which our behaviors worsen it. We focus on the threats that are visible and localized instead of those that are invisible and diffuse. We simplify complexity, draw a distinct line between good and evil, and dehumanize the enemy, much as our predecessors did with the Germans, the Japanese, and citizens of the former Soviet Union. We illustrate Reinhold Niebuhr's assessment of the human condition as framed by anxiety and the vain attempts to overcome it. We have become Niebuhr's man who climbs the mast of a ship during a storm at sea, unable to do otherwise yet terrified of the growing chasm beneath him.[2] Interesting times, to put it mildly.

And, in the midst of this, many people of faith feel called to be peacemakers. But what does peacemaking look like in this context? Should we carry Reinhold Niebuhr into this paragraph as well and say that peace requires a certain amount of coercion, given political reality? Or do we hold firm to the conviction that means and ends are organically related, such that one cannot achieve peace through violence? If we believe God to be the creator and sustainer of life, then

3

we know that the destruction of any life alienates us from God. If we believe God to be the *one* creator of *all* life, then we cannot assume that some lives have more value than others. And, if we believe that Jesus Christ reveals God's will to us, then we must take his words with utmost seriousness. "You have heard that it was said, 'An eye for an eye and a tooth for a tooth.' But I say to you, Do not resist one who is evil" (Matt. 5:38). And so my own United Methodist denomination joins others that declare war to be "incompatible with the teachings and example of Christ" and "reject war as a usual instrument of national foreign policy."[3]

These teachings seem so clear. For a minute I feel as certain as Leo Tolstoy, who insisted without wavering that one cannot be a Christian and support the use of violence. We may envision all kinds of scenarios in which this teaching is impractical, Tolstoy said. And we may devise more agreeable interpretations of Jesus' hard sayings. But we cannot deny that the law of nonresistance stands. In Tolstoy's words, "As a [person] cannot lift a mountain, and as a kindly [person] cannot kill an infant, so a [person] living the Christian life cannot take part in deeds of violence."[4]

Tolstoy felt the conflict between the law of God and the law of human beings so keenly that he believed that the Christian must withdraw from participation in society in order to live according to the teachings of Christ. He was not unique in his assessment and conclusion. Past and present are filled with people who live separately from the world in order to live faithfully to God. And even those of us who remain engaged in the world know the conflict that Tolstoy described. We are just more apt to refer to it as a tension, the tension between what God asks and what society requires.

Nearly one hundred years ago, Ernst Troeltsch described the ethos of the Christian faith as ongoing negotiation between ideals and history.[5] The interaction of the two pieces, faith and history, makes ethics possible. Indeed, the Christian moral life is precisely this: an ongoing negotiation between faith claims and lived experience. And this life is filled with moments in which a satisfying outcome to such negotiation seems out of reach. We find ourselves torn between conviction and circumstance. Let me be clear: I do not support the global war on terror currently waged by President Bush and his administration. I am not that torn. But I do see a world that is so broken that innocent people are in constant jeopardy. And I wonder if we can responsibly participate in this world without turning again to Niebuhr, who urged us to acknowledge the need for some violence in order to prevent our entire project from "issuing in complete disaster."[6]

What does it mean to be a peacemaker in this interesting era? How can we be responsible to a faith tradition that calls us to this vocation and be responsible to a world that is so fraught with violence that violence seems necessary?

Many of us who feel called to be peacemakers enter conversations on war by describing the rules, principles, and laws that bind us to an authority beyond the state. We cite Jesus' text on nonresistance or we cite the just-war tradition. Either way, our focus is on rules derived from a faith tradition and applied to this particular moment in history. While I do not mean to jettison these guiding principles of the faith, I do want to advocate for a different path. Instead of applying faith-based rules to this historical situation, can we think about infusing our personal activities with a religious sensibility? Can we begin to see our every action as a habit that cultivates a certain disposition? And can we try to identify and practice those habits that cultivate the disposition of peacemaker?[7]

## FROM PEACEMAKING TO PEACEBUILDING

We must acknowledge from the start that peacemaking has a negative connotation for some who associate the word with a shallow and superficial effort to "make nice" or "keep the peace." Such peacemaking shoves conflict under the rug, sets aside points of disagreement, and subdues calls for justice. We are reminded of the words of the prophet

Jeremiah, "You have healed the wounds of my people lightly, saying 'Peace, peace' when there is no peace." This kind of superficial calm is what we call "negative peace." It is the absence of conflict rather than the presence of justice. The underlying causes of conflict remain unaddressed. Surely, our call to labor for peace involves more than keeping the peace while injustice rages beneath the surface.

Peacemaking truly involves laboring for positive peace. Johan Galtung, a formative figure in peace and conflict studies, helped us with this definition by understanding violence to be much more than physical abuse. He described violence as anything that impedes one's ability to flourish. Violence is the cause of the difference between the potential and the actual, anything that prevents you from being who or what you could be. Positive peace is a similarly rich concept. Here, the underlying causes of violence and the persistent forms of injustice are addressed. Positive peace is not only the absence of violence, but also the presence of those conditions necessary for all people to realize their potential.[8]

Peacemaking does call us to this deeper, substantive effort. But the negative connotations are weighty enough to prevent many from envisioning the practice in this more athletic way. So, I suggest that we substitute the word "peacebuilding." Peacebuilding gets us away from the negative connotations of making peace as making nice. There is nothing superficial about the task of building peace because we need to think about the foundation, which means that we must unearth all of those things that make the project unstable. We have to deal with the hidden tensions, expose conflicts, and address their causes.

In this volume, Kathleen Greider and Elizabeth Conde-Frazier describe practices that do exactly that. From her field of pastoral care and counseling, Greider maps human tendencies regarding intercultural conflict so that we can see more clearly the obstacles and means to the nonviolent conflict that true peace and justice require. Conde-Frazier also addresses intercultural conflict, particularly between ethnic groups in congregational settings. She draws on literature from her field of religious education and on her experiences as a Latina minister to describe a series of practices beginning with hospitality and culminating in shalom. Both of these essays reflect an important truth about the task of peacebuilding, namely, that it is ongoing and cooperative in nature. The task never ends, nor can it be pursued in isolation. Peacebuilding requires the ethic of the cathedral builders that Bill Shore described in his book *The Cathedral Within.*[9] Here, we see people who are committed to labor for something that they know they will not realize. Building peace is like that. We build with and on the labor of others, contributing to a vision without assuming that we will be present for its completion.

## PEACEBUILDING AS A VIRTUE

Peacebuilding is not an occasional activity, but an ongoing effort. It involves practices performed not only as a response to needs in the world, but also as a means to character formation. Andrew Dreitcer's essay on prayer practices and my essay on the imagination illustrate this aspect of peacebuilding. Dreitcer demonstrates practices that integrate peacework into one's spiritual life, and I describe exercises that help us imagine alternatives to violence and to perceive connections to the other. Our essays reflect the belief that spirituality and the imagination bring sustenance and hope to peacebuilding *and* that our activities shape our inner life as well. We intend these prayer practices and imaginative exercises to further our spiritual growth as well as contribute to a world of peace. So, the peacework that we describe takes on the nature of a virtue in the classical sense, a habit that disposes us to act well, according to a suitable end.

We owe this definition to Aristotle although St. Thomas Aquinas wove it into the Christian tradition. Aristotle understood the highest good (that end desired for its own sake and not as a means to something else) to be *eudaimonia,* translated imperfectly as happiness but meaning well-being and well-doing. The highest good of all human action and effort, as Aristotle understood it, is a sort of functional excellence, whereby the human being perfectly performs the function of being human. Our pursuit of this ultimate end is aided by the intellectual and moral virtues, which dispose us to act well according to that end of functional excellence.

Aquinas's understanding of the end carried the mark of Augustine, meaning that he understood the highest good to be more than natural happiness or functional excellence. According to Aquinas, the highest good is supernatural happiness or union with God. And we cannot pursue this end with the moral and intellectual virtues alone. We also need virtues that are infused in us by God and orient us toward God. These are the theological virtues: faith, hope, and love.[10] While I have no doubt that faith, hope, and love are intimately linked to the habit of peacebuilding, I am not bold enough to add peacebuilding to the triad of theological virtues. But I do think we can speak of peacebuilding as a moral virtue with some integrity.

Aristotle and Aquinas taught that moral virtues are "formed by habit." We are, by nature, "equipped with the ability to receive" the moral virtues, writes Aristotle, but "habit brings this ability to completion and fulfillment." Therefore, his teaching in *Nicomachean Ethics* continues, "We become just by the practice of just actions, self-controlled by exercising self-control, and courageous by performing acts of courage."[11] The opposite holds true also. We acquire bad, unjust, fearful, indulgent habits by performing those kinds of actions. In sum, "the actions determine what kind of characteristics are developed."[12] This means that moral virtues are not acquired by performing any kind of action, but only by performing those actions which a virtuous person would perform.

We refer to these actions as practices.[13] A practice is an action performed repeatedly so that it cultivates a particular disposition. For the sake of clarity, let us unpack this definition before returning to the particular disposition of peacebuilding. First, the word "action" is not intended to distinguish a practice from reflection. Indeed, as we will see shortly, reflection is part of practice, not separate from it. By action, we really mean any form of activity, any thing that one does. It does not require a certain amount of movement. Nor does it require a public forum. In other words, action may include but is not restricted to activism. Thus, some of the practices described here are meditative and solitary while others involve more movement in a public sphere. A practice is any form of activity.

And yet, in another sense, a practice is not just any form of activity, but one that is deliberately chosen. It is an action intended to cultivate a particular disposition. Here, we see that a practice requires reflection. The action is deliberately chosen because of the effect it will produce. We then reflect on the experience of performing the activity and on its effect in order to determine if and how to repeat the activity. Frank Rogers and Carol Lakey Hess illustrate such reflection on practice in their essays on narrative arts and just discourse, respectively. Rogers shares stories created by young people grappling with the call to love their enemies in this world of fear and hatred. It is the practice of creating these stories (as much as staging and sharing them) that enables one to question, challenge, and envision. Lakey Hess also reflects on a dialogical practice, focusing on the tension between advocacy and dialogue. She maps practices that foster peacebuilding classrooms, places where individuals use dialogue, a nonviolent means, to develop and promote visions of shalom via advocacy. Rogers and Lakey Hess recommend these particular practices because they have seen their effect on young people who learn empathy and on classroom participants who engage one another in genuine and constructive conversation. These essays, therefore, nicely illustrate our capacity to choose practices that cultivate a particular disposition.

We may not expect the practice to either initiate or complete the disposition, but we do expect the practice to reinforce a habit. We must, after all, be disposed toward something before we would begin practicing it. So, the practice cannot initiate the disposition; it is rather a response to this inclination. But we do recognize that our inclination needs to be reinforced, and we identify forms of activity that would reinforce it. The essay immediately following this introduction develops these points using the language of vocation. Philip Amerson and John Woell describe vocation as "faithfully bringing together our ritual life and our ethical life." It involves striving to find and practice daily disciplines that give full expression to our faith, and the Christian faith calls for a witness and discipline of peacebuilding.

This language of vocation reminds us that the disposition or the discipline is not itself the end. We are not called to a practice for its own sake, but rather for the effect it promises in our life and world. I have a friend who is very intentional about what she eats, wears, and buys. I respect her convictions tremendously. But she admits to a tendency to lose the vision for the virtues. That is, she becomes so focused on habits that she loses sight of their larger purpose, which really is not about her at all. Through peacebuilding practices, we do want to cultivate a particular disposition in ourselves. But there is also a goal that stretches far beyond us. In a very real sense, we want to make ourselves instruments of peace, to use St. Francis's lovely phrase. That is, we offer our bodies for the purpose of crafting a world that is less violent and more loving. We need to tune the instrument not for its own sake, but for the part it plays in the symphony.

This collaborative project does not constitute a symphony, but the instruments gathered here do make a nice ensemble. After Amerson and Woell's chapter on the vocation of peacebuilding, the remaining chapters unfold as follows. First come the pieces by Dreitcer, Marshall, and Rogers, which share a certain creative sensibility, expressed through prayer, visioning and meditation, and story-telling, respectively. Although each of these also incorporates a social element, the practices begin with an individual spiritual or imaginative exercise. Next come the essays by Lakey Hess, Greider, and Conde-Frazier, which begin with reflection on a social experience, though the settings vary from classroom to community to congregation. They then describe practices for individuals in these settings, thus changing personal habits and transforming contexts simultaneously. Gathered together, these essays present a range of practices that exercise different aspects of inner life and engage different social settings and concerns. Although our reach is in no way comprehensive, we do rejoice in its breadth and the potential for all readers to find something meaningful here.

## CONCLUSION

Our focus on practices does not simplify these interesting times. We continue to struggle with the demands of conscience and society and feel daunted by the call to peacebuilding. But a focus on practices is helpful (and thus worth commending) for two main reasons. Primarily, this emphasis on practice is empowering. Recent events have left many of us feeling utterly powerless. Even the outpouring of opposition at governmental and grassroots levels could not stop the Bush administration from bombing Baghdad in March 2003. An emphasis on practices is empowering not because it convinces us that our actions will have their intended effect. Rather, an emphasis on practices is empowering precisely because it infuses an action with a meaning that is not solely contingent on its effect on the world. As a practice, the act has meaning in and of itself. This does not mean that effect does not matter, but it does mean that effect is not the only thing that matters. For example, it is important that I write a letter to President Bush even though he will not read it. The act itself has value. I am no longer paralyzed by the question: is it possible to be a peacebuilder in a world that so easily convinces us of the necessity for violence? Of course it is. We become peacebuilders by practicing peace. The practice itself has value.

In classical terms, a practice has value because it disposes us to act in a certain way. This brings us to the second great contribution of practices language: it reminds us that we become what we do. Character is formed, not implanted. This idea is certainly familiar to those of us in the United Methodist tradition and any faith that has been influenced by pietism. We do our best to abide by the teachings of Christ not because we have to, but because we see this life as a striving toward Christ-like behavior. Our faith tradition does provide us with rules that proscribe the use of violence and with visions of a time when no one will hurt or destroy in all God's holy mountain. But peacebuilding requires more than abiding by rules and articulating visions. It also requires practices whereby we cultivate the disposition of peacebuilding. We need to infuse our every action with this kind of meaning, to see each act as contributing to the kind of person we are becoming. In the beautifully succinct words of a great peacebuilder, Mahatma Gandhi, we must be the change we wish to see.

## NOTES

1. Albert Camus, *Resistance, Rebellion, and Death* (New York: Vintage International, 1995), 249.

2. Reinhold Niebuhr, *The Nature and Destiny of Man*, vol. 1: *Human Nature* (New York: Charles Scribner's Sons, 1964), 185.

3. *The Social Principles of the United Methodist Church — 2000* (Nashville: United Methodist Publishing House, 2000), ¶165.

4. Leo Tolstoy, "Letter to Ernest Howard Crosby," in *Approaches to Peace: A Reader in Peace Studies*, ed. David Barash (New York: Oxford University Press, 2000), 178.

5. Ernst Troeltsch, *The Social Teaching of the Christian Churches*, vol. 2, reprint (Louisville: Westminster/John Knox, 1992), 1004–6.

6. Reinhold Niebuhr, *Moral Man and Immoral Society: A Study in Ethics and Politics*, 1st Touchstone ed. (New York: Simon & Schuster, 1995), 22.

7. Although our suggestions for practices are different, we do share the motivation of those scholars, activists, and church people involved in just-peace movements, and I want to acknowledge their important work. As Glen Stassen has written, they too are working to ensure that our approach to war and peace involves more than the single dimension of a pacifism–just war debate. Stassen and his colleagues map a second dimension of just-peace practices. See Glen Stassen, ed., *Just Peacemaking: Ten Practices for Abolishing War* (Cleveland: Pilgrim Press, 1998). For more recent reflections, including this language of two-dimensional ethics, see Glen Stassen, "The Unity, Reason, and Obligatoriness of Just Peacemaking Theory," *Journal of the Society of Christian Ethics* 23, no. 1 (Spring–Summer 2003): 171–97. This volume also contains a comprehensive bibliography of just-peace resources.

8. Johan Galtung, "Violence and Peace," in *A Reader in Peace Studies,* ed. Paul Smoker, Ruth Davies, and Barbara Munske (Oxford: Pergamon Press, 1990), 9–14.

9. Bill Shore, *The Cathedral Within: Transforming Your Life by Giving Something Back* (New York: Random House, 1999).

10. See Thomas Aquinas, *Treatise on the Virtues,* trans. John A. Oesterle (Notre Dame, Ind.: University of Notre Dame Press, 1966).

11. Aristotle, *Nicomachean Ethics,* trans. Martin Ostwald (Englewood Cliffs, N.J.: Prentice Hall, 1962), 2.1.1103b.

12. Ibid., 2.2.1103b.30.

13. For a more formal discussion of the link between practice and virtue, see Alasdair MacIntyre, *After Virtue* (Notre Dame, Ind.: University of Notre Dame Press, 1984). We also want to acknowledge the work of Dorothy C. Bass and her colleagues. Although our use of the word "practices" is broader, we do see compatibility between their rich projects and ours.

See Dorothy C. Bass, ed., *Practicing Our Faith: A Way of Life for a Searching People* (San Francisco: Jossey-Bass, 1997), and Dorothy C. Bass and Miroslav Volf, eds., *Practicing Theology: Beliefs and Practices in Christian Life* (Grand Rapids: Eerdmans, 2001).

# CHAPTER ONE

# THE VOCATION OF PEACEBUILDING

*Philip A. Amerson and John W. Woell*

It seems that committed Christians have not yet fully decided how to bear witness as peacemakers to the abiding specter of warfare. In our world of terrorism, tyranny, and tragedy, a commitment to a pacifist stance does not seem to come readily. This question of how we respond to war has been very much alive since at least the time of Augustine and has found diverse expression in pillars of the Christian faith like Aquinas, Luther, Calvin, and Wesley. Our concern here is to find resources in contemporary reflections on the Christian faith for living up to our calling as peacemakers within the larger world community. Recent events have made the need for such exploration all the more pressing.

Traditionally, the church has espoused two positions: pacifism and just war. The former holds that it is impossible in principle to justify any war at all. Whether one's grounds for taking such a principled stand are moral or religious, as a pacifist one refuses to bear arms and questions the justifications of those who do. The latter holds that war cannot be waged indiscriminately but that, under certain circumstances, war is permissible between states. Through the application of specific criteria to particular situations, one may come to a reasoned and justified endorsement of military action.[1] However, that these are simply two extremes that form the ends of a continuum is perhaps more obvious now than ever. What is evident in contemporary literature is the difficulty of finding a way to mediate between these seemingly divergent — if not diametrically opposed — sets of principles, both of which inform the tradition in which we operate.

When the United Methodist Council of Bishops sought to make a statement concerning war and violence at their fall gathering in November 2001, the resulting stir across the denomination showed the power of retaliatory thinking in many circles in the church. Those who believe that some ethical groundwork, other than retribution, should have been laid before establishing national policy were rudely awakened by the fact that the Bush administration, with heavy support from the public, acknowledged few ethical dilemmas in entering a preemptive and protracted military effort. Methodist persons of faith, who sincerely seek to live out the denomination's Disciplinary precepts on war, have often been overcome by retaliatory thinking of their own as efforts to increase the United States' national security have surged forward in the last few years.

How have Christian churches as a whole responded to these recent decisions to use the United States' military might? It is too soon to say. In many places there seem to be remarkable new energies and insights for living and speaking in ways that will build peace even in an age of terror. And yet we have ideological wars *within* the church. One might rightly ask why we would presume to say anything to the political and military structures beyond the church when we have not yet found ways to bring a process for reconciliation into play in our many internal ideological wars. If we cannot find a voice on our common calling to be peacemakers, whatever method we would prefer, of what use are we to anyone, even ourselves?

Theodore R. Weber brings to the table a remarkably helpful notion when he writes: "A Christian's decision with regard to war is made *in statu confessionis* — an expression of one's confession of faith, one's calling. . . . [T]he confessional state is the *vocation of peacemaking* and not the person's stand with regard to war and participation."[2] What matters is that we recognize that our own confessions of Christian faith provide the context within which decisions regarding war and participation are made. This, then, points the way to our suggestion of how we might respond: to seek *to practice among ourselves the vocation of peacebuilding.*

Such practice, the full living of such a vocation, has been approached in myriad ways by diverse thinkers. As mentioned above, historical investigations reveal an ongoing debate regarding the virtues of pacifist or just-war doctrines for the church at large. More recently, discussion has turned to the examination of the practices of the church in hopes of finding some unified stance on war. But such investigations, though historically and academically interesting, fail to guide us when the question of whether or not we will support or participate in a particular military action presses in upon us. Such investigations reveal that the vocation of peacebuilding is a lived vocation incorporating the concerns of both pacifism and just war and permeating the life of the believer, whether military action is distant or imminent. The vocation of peacebuilding is not a place in which one rests on principles but in which one engages dynamically with the world.

## THE CHURCH AND THE QUESTION OF WAR

So that our own churches not escape scrutiny, we want, in this section of the essay, to offer the United Methodist Church as a historical example of the ways in which the church has struggled with questions of military involvement in the past; in the next section, we speak briefly of the Evangelical Lutheran Church in America's statements regarding war in general and the recent military action in Iraq. United Methodist documents over the course of the last sixty-five years reveal a church that, like many others, is struggling to come to terms with the principles of pacifism and just war. As with other mainline denominations, there has been a certain theological ebb and flow to United Methodism's stance on war through the tumultuous twentieth century. This denomination serves as a particularly poignant example because of its constant reevaluation of doctrines and the prominence of its discussions on questions of pacifism and just war.

At the Uniting Conference of 1939 several branches of American Methodism (Methodist Episcopal North, Methodist Episcopal South, and Methodist Protestant) were brought together again as the Methodist Church. At these sessions a forceful and direct statement against war for any cause was made in a document known as the "undivided stance." This declaration was rooted in long-endorsed proclamations written prior to union by these merging Methodists, and it was also, no doubt, shaped by a concern to keep the United States from joining the war already raging in Europe. That there were pacifist leanings and intentions within each of these branches of the Methodist family tree and reflected in many of their premerger documents is clear.[3] However, language sympathetic to a nonviolent stance in the documents from the 1939 Uniting Conference and in the 1940 General Conference proceedings virtually disappears in the 1944 *Book of Discipline*.

D. Stephen Long argued in *Living the Discipline* that United Methodism, at least through the 1992 General Conference, was constitutionally if not practically a pacifist denomination. He observed that through her constitution (*Confession of Faith*, Article XVI), *Social Principles*, and paragraphs dealing with the role of pastors as counselors in times of war, the denomination was by charter committed to pacifism. However, Long had to admit that in practice the denomination was not then and had not up to that time functioned as a pacifist church.[4]

Long's assertions regarding the written documents of the denomination seem to be on solid ground. Article 16, paragraph 68, of the constitutional *Confession of Faith* in *The Book of Discipline of the United Methodist Church* contains these remarkable words: "We believe war and bloodshed are contrary to the gospel and spirit of Christ. We believe it is the duty of Christian citizens to give moral strength and purpose to their respective governments through sober, righteous, and godly living."[5] Woven into the very fabric of Methodist beliefs is a concise statement of what appears to be a pacifist stance.

However, Long also makes a strong case that pacifism, while it was always deeply embedded in the warp and woof of these twentieth-century followers of Wesley, was also ephemeral, was not uniformly affirmed, and was subject to being diminished in times of war or when it did not suit the larger purposes of bringing the paternalistic values of American civilization to the world. That is, pacifism, as a set of abstract principles, could be applied or ignored as the situation dictated. Getting from theory to practice proved difficult at best.

Shifts in disciplinary language, like those made between 1939 and 1944, continue into the current era. At the 2000 General Conference of the United Methodist Church in Cleveland, Ohio, there was extended and vigorous debate in legislative sessions regarding the paragraphs on war in *The Social Principles* (Paragraph 165C and Paragraph 164G). At stake was the hope of many persons like Stephen Long that the language of the church would continue to be language that excluded the possibility of justifying war in any circumstance. At this General Conference, for the first time in American Methodist history there was an acknowledgment that most Christians have accepted the just-war doctrine. *The Social Principles*, Paragraph 165C (previously Paragraph 69C) in *The 2000 Book of Discipline of the United Methodist Church* read: "We therefore reject war as the *usual* instrument of national policy." Prior to this, *The Social Principles* were clear that there was an unqualified rejection of "war as an instrument of national foreign policy."[6] There is, nonetheless, clear provision made in the paragraphs of the 2000 *Discipline* pertaining to the support the church is to give persons who seek to be conscientious objectors to war.

Although Long makes a compelling case that an inclination to pacifism is deeply embedded in Methodist and United Brethren antecedents, more recent actions by succeeding General Conferences have not conformed with Long's vision that through discipline and teaching God may "raise up people who will provide a vision of holiness to cultivate in us the virtue of peace."[7] Not only does there seem to be some division between Long's vision for the church and the denomination's own documents, but there is considerable debate over the very resources on which Long would draw in formulating his pacifist vision for the United Methodist Church.

In *Politics in the Order of Salvation,* Theodore Weber charges that Long and others have mistakenly inferred that the church was officially pacifist by action of the General Conference.[8] After careful review of a wide range of source materials Weber concludes: "The Wesleyan position, insofar as the reference is to John Wesley himself, is the just war ethic. It is not pacifism, and it most certainly is not a martial, nationalistic crusading spirit. However, Wesley's just-war position is not doctrinally necessary for Methodist Christians. Neither is any other attitude toward war."[9] Weber notes that prominent leaders in the early Methodist movement held strong and contradictory views regarding military service and participation in war. Based on clearly pacifist theological arguments, John Nelson, one of Wesley's most trusted preachers, was prepared to be imprisoned rather than be inscribed into military service. On the other hand, John Fletcher, the designated successor to Wesley, argued in favor of the use of the sword to pursue the just causes of the state.[10]

Reviewing these materials from within the Methodist tradition leaves us with several questions. There is the historical question for the Methodist Church: was there a trajectory in Wesley's thought that, were he living today, might have resulted in an embrace of either a pacifist or a just-war position? There is the methodological question for the historians: is such a question, filled as it is with anachronistic assumptions, of any value to us at all? Questions such as these arise of necessity when pursuing projects like Long's or Weber's.

Seeking to answer such historical and methodological questions pushes us back to the more general dilemma with which we must wrestle as Christians: what is to be said of the traditional doctrines of pacifism and just war in our contemporary context? This forces itself upon us when we recognize that such realities as a constitutionally based, democratic nation-state and the development of indiscriminate nuclear and biological weaponry were not a part of Wesley's range of experience and are of such importance that it is difficult to factor them into any formula to determine what Wesley might think about war to-day. Would Wesley choose pacifism? Steve Long might argue "yes," and Ted Weber would likely say "no." In reviewing these historical documents and studies, one can see the witness of hundreds of Methodist believers seeking to live faithfully as followers of Christ. Nearly identical struggles could be traced through the documents of other mainline denominations.[11]

That there can be a plurality of opinions on this question should push us in a new direction; it should push us to wonder what sort of impact the answer to this question might have on the practices of Methodists in particular and Christians in general. There are many pathways open so that individuals or churches can be pacifist in multiple ways or those who believe in just-war doctrines can act to reduce violence and seek to channel warfare toward just ends. The range of nonviolent alternatives seems limited only by one's imagination.

## PROBLEMS OF PRINCIPLES AND PRACTICES

Pacifism has typically not been passivity nor has commitment to a just-war stance been *ipso facto* an endorsement of violence. Our history stretches out for review like a palimpsest set on a table before us. There are remnants of nearly erased passages that still can be seen on the page. We review the material and are still left with the question, "What shall we say about participation in war?" That is, as academically interesting as the questions posed in the previous section are, their answers may not provide the kind of clarity or sense of direction sought in the ambiguous circumstances we face. What we require in order to fulfill a calling to be peacemakers is a direct answer to the question,

"How do we build peace in *this* violent world?" Although historical considerations can certainly be brought to bear, the answer to this question is a decidedly moral one.

The difficulties with Long's project of looking for the principled stance of the United Methodist Church are neither simply historical nor limited to its singular focus on responding to war and violence. The difficulty with ethics in general, and with any ethic based on adherence to principles in particular, has long been recognized. Aristotle's *Nicomachean Ethics* puts the problem this way: "[M]ost people . . . take refuge in theory and think they are being philosophers and will become good in this way, behaving somewhat like patients who listen attentively to their doctors, but do none of the things they are ordered to do. As the latter will not be made well in body by such a course of treatment, the former will not be made well in soul by such a course of philosophy."[12] One must be able to apply the theory in order for it to do one's soul any good. The theory must find its way into practice. Likewise, when it comes to discussions of moral principles, the search for principles by which one might act morally is at most half the task. *Phronēsis*, or practical reason, requires that such principles find application in particular situations and that the ends of such applications vary depending upon those situations.

The challenge of applying a principle is illustrated by the "Social Statement on For Peace in God's World" of the Evangelical Lutheran Church in America (ELCA). Although explicitly affirming the just-war doctrine that has been part of the Lutheran tradition for centuries, the statement follows this affirmation with these words:

> In doing so, we face conflicting moral claims and agonizing dilemmas. Helping the neighbor in need may require protecting innocent people from injustice and aggression. While we support the use of nonviolent measures, there may be no other way to offer protection in some circumstances than by restraining forcibly those harming the innocent. We do not, then — for the sake of

the neighbor — rule out possible support for the use of military force. We must determine in particular circumstances whether or not military action is the lesser evil.[13]

The statement itself recognizes that the adherence to principles does not give one rest; rather, much deliberation must take place before it is clear whether or not the principles themselves can be applied to a particular set of circumstances.

Tellingly, in a statement on the recent war against Iraq, ELCA Presiding Bishop Mark S. Hanson, having cited the failure of the Bush administration to gain the consent of the United Nations for military action in the Middle East, chose not to quote the above words or others that would show the relationship between this particular situation and just-war principles. Rather, he chose yet another passage from that same statement: "We also affirm that governments should vigorously pursue less coercive measures over more coercive ones: consent over compulsion, nonviolence over violence, diplomacy over military engagement, and deterrence over war."[14] In this instance, the explicit affirmation of just-war principles has given way to considerations that would sound familiar to the pacifist. A community of believers that adheres to just-war principles has recognized that such principles are not an end in themselves. Rather, they are but one expression of the vocation of peacebuilding that forms our faith.

If we return to the United Methodist Church, the most focused effort made in recent years to answer questions about participation in war came in the document *In Defense of Creation,* prepared as a pastoral letter from the bishops of the church on how to deal with the then-looming threat of nuclear war between the United States and the U.S.S.R. It is a stunningly powerful witness to how we must live in the face of the enormous nuclear stockpiles that resulted from cold-war tensions. Although prepared within the context of the cold war and the nuclear arms race that marked its last three decades, this letter wrestles with difficulties germane to both pacifist and just-war stances decades later.

One intriguing response to the bishops' letter came from Paul Ramsey and Stanley Hauerwas in the book *Speak Up for Just War or Pacifism.*[15] Ramsey and Hauerwas, representing the pluralism that has been a part of Methodism since the time of Fletcher and Nelson, levy a powerful critique against the analysis done in the bishops' letter and pronounce it to be lacking in ethical and political substance. While there is not sufficient space in this chapter to review those arguments, the most important concern raised by Ramsey and Hauerwas is that the bishops did not give adequate attention to the question of how the leaders of the church would speak to the church. To Ramsey and Hauerwas this came first — clarity as to what should be said to those in pulpit and pew. Rather than seeking to speak a prophetic word to the world, the bishops should have helped the people in local parishes to see how they might wrestle with the questions of pacifism or just war and be converted to behaving as peacemakers in the world. Moving as the bishops' discussion of principles was, their failure to attend adequately to practices weakened their position considerably.

Whatever one makes of their particular arguments for pacifism and just war as resources upon which Christians must draw in formulating practices of peace and understanding their vocation, the comments of Bishop Hanson and the critical work of Ramsey and Hauerwas highlight the hard moral questions that arise when the Christian faith runs up against political and military reality. Just as there seems to be no consensus on a single "Methodist" or "Lutheran" stance on war, so too is there no consensus on a single "Christian" stance on war. What is most interesting to us about the plurality of opinions is the assumption that they share: namely, that there ought to be at least a denominational if not a Christian stance on war to be found between the alternatives of pacifism and just war. It seems to us that although searching for a Christian doctrine on war can bear fruit, it is unlikely to bear the fruit for which we would hope. The power of Bishop Hanson's statement and of Ramsey and Hauerwas's critique lies precisely in this point. The principles alone, without a clear plan for implementation, or a clear set of complementary practices, are simply too thin, too pliable.

Further, the times of crisis in which deliberations over doctrines such as pacifism and just war become most important are the very times at which such deliberations are unlikely to take place. In the aftermath of the destruction of the World Trade Center in New York City, many of us were stunned at the saliency of other, not so noble, deeply embedded patterns within our churches and culture. The remarkably swift and seemingly uncritical move that was made to embrace retaliation and revenge in the culture at large, and in many parishes in particular, was breathtaking to those who had assumed that any endorsement of military action would be tested by the classic just-war principles. Others, who had begun to believe that a new set of principles calling for a just-peace[16] doctrine would be considered in discussions within the press and church, were also astonished at the urgings to "strike back" and "punish someone — anyone" for the terror. Once again we see the blinding power of fear at work in shaping public policy.

Weber helps us to see the way around such problems by returning once again to the considerations of his historical study:

> What is essential in Wesley's tradition is that one's stance with regard to war and military participation be placed in the context of the vocation of peacemaking. For the just war ethic, that means an emphasis on the criterion of just intention — which requires that war move toward the re-creation of political community and therefore toward a just and healing peace. For pacifism, it means serious attention to the requirement of peace as the organization of power.[17]

Weber makes clear that the question of how to live out one's vocation as a peacemaker remains open whether one has decided upon a pacifist *or* a just-war stance. The tenets of these two doctrines are not of central importance. Rather, what matters for Christians is their commitment to the vocation of peacebuilding first and foremost. Pacifism, just war, and just peace are but three expressions of this vocation.

## VOCATION — OPENNESS TO THE THIN PLACES

The material rehearsed thus far brings two points into focus. First, neither historical nor moral considerations of principles of pacifism and just war alone are adequate to a Christian calling of peacemaking. Second, attention to the implementation of these principles needs to be specific, circumstantial, and critical. Our suggestion has been that discussions of principles cannot offer us much help when the question of war presses in on us. By the time the situations arise in which such principles might be invoked, there is little time for reflection upon them.

How then are we to live out the vocation of peacebuilding? How are we to build peace in a violent world if adherence to the principles of either pacifism or just war is not enough? It seems that Christians must look for other resources in the Christian life and practice that can be of aid. The deliberations of the United Methodist Church, Long's and Weber's discussions of the principles of pacifism and just war, Bishop Hanson's comments on the war against Iraq, and Ramsey and Hauerwas's critique of the Bishop's letter each reveal in their own way the need for some understanding of the context in which the principles of pacifism and just war have their meaning. If this context is that of the lived Christian life, then looking at either pacifism or just war in that context ought to reveal something about that life as it is reflected in these principles. In fact, we would argue that close attention to these principles and the discussions of them above reveals that the Christian life as a whole is a vocation dedicated to building peace and that these sets of principles themselves and discussions of them are but different expressions of this vocation. Given the diversity of contexts in which faithful people live and the many positions on the question of war that seem to be available to them, it would be unwise, if not impossible, for us to offer yet another set of principles through which one may live out this vocation. Rather, we offer the following reflections on and examples of the vocation of peacebuilding.

Vocation is not about seeking to please or impress; rather, it is about faithfully bringing together our ritual life and our ethical life. In Wesley's language, it is holding acts of piety and acts of mercy together in faithful witness. Vocation is the call to find the daily disciplines that are congruent with a baptismal and Eucharistic center. As such, vocation is a communal expression of a deeply rooted grammar for our living. Brad Kallenberg explores such continuities and dissonances in the thought of Ludwig Wittgenstein and Stanley Hauerwas and suggests that it is in concrete and daily practices that there is the cultivation of "skillful engagement in Christian discourse."[18] Our daily lives reveal the depths of our understanding of the Christian faith itself. We engage in Christian discourse skillfully when our practices reveal clearly this grammar of Christian living.

This skill is not the skill of following a technique but of engaging in a practice. Kallenberg writes: "[B]ecause moral reasoning and Christian praxis are conceived as internally related, theological ethics is revealed to be none other than an explication of the form of life of the actual community, which is to say the grammar of Christian discourse."[19] If the Christian form of life is indeed a form of life lived out in practices of building peace, then it should come as no surprise that the grammar of this discourse is the grammar of peace. When we read statements from either those who adhere to pacifist principles or those who adhere to just-war principles, it must be recognized that these statements share this grammar. Worked out from within the Christian form of life, both doctrines simply are explications of that life.

As noted above, Weber points to peacemaking in the Wesleyan spirit as a vocational concept that "is the very nature of the calling to gain the mind of Christ in all things."[20] Further, he asserts, "The vocation of peacemaker is one that Christian believers cannot decline without losing the peace of God, and with it their sure knowledge of good and their ability to resist the power of sin."[21] To be a Christian is simply to be called to build peace. The failure to recognize this calling is a failure at the very heart of one's Christian faith — a failure that could carry dire consequences. It is to abandon the grammar within Christian life and to live senselessly.

An examination of writings from diverse Christian traditions can reveal that the Christian form of life is explicated through a grammar of peacemaking. Wesley spoke of *Inward Holiness* and *Outward Holiness* and was not willing to separate the two. Perhaps this is why we struggle with his understandings of peacemaking. In the language of the Quakers, "If you want peace, begin by practicing peace." Seeking peace is not only an end but also the means by which that end is pursued; the means and the ends are internally related.[22]

Wesley's reflections on the term "peacemaker" from his sermon on the beatitude in Matthew 5, "blessed are the peacemakers for they shall be called the children of God," bring the breadth and depth of the vocation of peacebuilding to the fore:

> Hence we may easily learn in how wide a sense the term "peacemakers" is to be understood. In its literal meaning it implies those lovers of God and man who utterly detest and abhor all strife and debate, all variance and contention; and accordingly labour with all their might either to prevent this fire of hell from being kindled, or when it is kindled from breaking out, or when it is broke out from spreading farther. They endeavor to calm the stormy spirits of men, to quiet their turbulent passions, to soften the minds of contending parties, and if possible reconcile them to each other. They use all innocent arts, and employ all their strength, all the talents which God has given them, as well to preserve peace where it is and to restore it where it is not. It is the joy of their heart to promote, to confirm, to increase mutual goodwill among men, but more especially among the children of God, however distinguished by things of smaller importance; that as they have all "one

Lord, one faith," *as they are all "called in one hope of their calling," so
they may all walk "worthy of the vocation wherewith they are called;*
with all lowliness and meekness, with long-suffering, forbearing
one another in love; endeavoring to keep the unity of the Spirit
in the bond of peace."[23]

If peacemaking is a calling, a vocation, then how ought we live? In
truth one may never fully know, or as St. Paul suggests, "For now I
know in part, but then I shall know just as I am also known." But this
is entirely the point: the vocation of peacemaking reveals itself slowly
and over time in a life lived in that vocation.

From a very different quarter of the theological universe, Father
Ronald Rolheiser asks what spiritual practices are essential. He then
identifies "The Essentials of a Christian Spirituality." Rolheiser, who
is writing more than 250 years after Wesley, from a Roman Catholic
perspective based on a phenomenological search for these "essentials"
and with no apparent reference to knowledge of John Wesley's work,
arrives at the "Four Nonnegotiable Pillars of the Spiritual Life."[24] What
is remarkable is that these four practices are almost exact parallels to
the four elements of the *General Rule of Discipleship* laid out for Methodist followers by John Wesley. While Wesley spoke of (1) devotion,
(2) worship, (3) justice, and (4) charity, or compassion, Rolheiser "discovers" (1) private prayer, (2) communities of true worship, (3) social
justice, and (4) mellowness of heart (compassion).[25] Peace is both the
means and the end of the Christian vocation.

If peacebuilding is at the heart of our vocation, then there is much
yet to learn from our sacramental and disciplined daily practices about
how to live this calling. Persons like Tex Sample have been urging
Christians to discover a renewed Christian stance for justice based on
the Eucharist and Baptism.[26] He suggests that embedded deep in these
ritual acts is the performance of justice. Here, each time we receive
the bread and cup and each time we stand with one who is newly
baptized we are claiming our vocation as peacemakers. We are called

to be a part of God's ongoing incarnation in a broken world, and this is why we practice the sacraments. As Robert McAfee Brown wrote: "In a sacrament, life is, for a single moment the way it is supposed to be in all moments."[27] The life of peace is experienced fully, if only for a moment, in the practice of the sacraments themselves. Alan Jones expresses it thus: "The sacraments (particularly baptism and the Eucharist) are the story in action. They are food for pilgrims as they try to find their way through the labyrinth of human experience. The two great maps for Christians are the Bible and sacraments."[28] William T. Cavanaugh tells of the salience of the Eucharist in the face of the dictatorship of Pinochet in Chile. He argues that it was in the sacraments that the most prophetic actions of nonviolent resistance were possible. The Eucharist became, according to Cavanaugh, the most important signal for declaring that the torturers would not ultimately win and that love was more powerful than hate. It was not a passive act; torturers were denied access to the sacrament unless there was genuine and lived repentance.[29] New community was possible through an ancient ritual brought to bear as people gathered to practice their true vocation.

Reflections such as these simply reveal that the Christian is called to a vocation of peacebuilding and that one is strengthened toward a daily life of faithful discovery through practiced faithful living. To think of building peace as one's Christian vocation is to recognize how embedded the practice of peacemaking is within the Christian story. Given the difficulties with thinking of peacemaking either as adherence to the principles of pacifism or just war or as particular actions performed for external ends, the notion of vocationally shaped identities recommends itself as a dynamic way to approach the vexing question of how one responds to violence and oppression in our world. We can recognize discussions of pacifism and of just war as various attempts to speak to this vocation. We can then live in and for peace. When situations arise that require a response to violence, our response will be at the ready because we will already be living it. In our thinking, in our speaking, and in our acting as well as in our participation in the sacraments, we will be consciously fulfilling our vocation of building peace. This vocation is revealed to be the very context in which the Christian faith is lived.

## CONCLUSION

The story of how we will respond to violence is one derived from many communities and many individuals who have sought to live faithfully. This history affirms the idea that if we are to desire peace we must live it. Wesley was committed to peacemaking, but he was also a child of his times and of his social position. For those of us who would be "practical" in our "theology" there is the need to speak the story of peace to one another within our churches and through our rituals. This story of reconciliation may appear to be hidden, but it is as close as the sacraments we share and the memories of peacemakers we hold dear. By practicing, communities of peace may, from time to time, uncover a deeply vested grammar of love that will surprise us and, upon occasion, shine through our everyday encounters, lighting the way before us for a lifetime.

## NOTES

1. The just-war criteria and interpretations of them have continually been shaped since the times of St. Augustine and St. Thomas Aquinas. This doctrine is meant to control and severely limit warfare. The tenets of this doctrine suggest that any and all just wars must:

- have a *just cause* seeking justice in response to serious evil;
- have a *just intention* for the restoration of peace with justice, and must not seek self-enrichment or devastation of another nation;
- be the *last resort;*
- have *legitimate authority* with war being declared only by properly constituted government; and
- have a *reasonable hope of success.*

Even more to the point in our current crisis, the just-war position suggests that if war should break out, such fighting must be constrained by two principles:

- *Discrimination:* respect is to be shown for the rights of enemy peoples and immunity given to noncombatants from direct attack.

- *Proportionality:* whereby the amount of damage inflicted must be proportionate to the ends sought. A war's harm must not exceed the war's good.

It is important to note that both the decision-making criteria and the constraints that follow once these criteria have been met are formulated so as to emphasize the need for thoughtful consideration of how these criteria might be fulfilled by a particular situation. Interestingly, all the criteria for a just war may be met without resulting in any form of military action. It may be the case that the first five criteria are fulfilled by a particular situation but that it is impossible to act in that situation in a way that fulfills these latter two criteria, for example, if any military action were to result in damages disproportionate to the good that might result. Thus, these principles serve less as principles that can be invoked at will and more as a program for more work. (See note 16 below for one such development of this doctrine.)

2. Theodore R. Weber, *Politics in the Order of Salvation: New Directions in Wesleyan Political Ethics* (Nashville: Kingswood Books, 2001), 387 (emphasis added).

3. For a fine review of these documents see D. Stephen Long, *Living the Discipline* (Grand Rapids: W. B. Eerdmans, 1992), 52–62. Pastors who were conscientious objectors to the world wars were nurtured into their faith. They did not arise *de novo*. Such persons were shaped by a deep and widening stream of pacifist sentiment in the church during the early decades of the twentieth century. There were strong pacifist voices among the administration and faculty of the Methodist and other colleges in those decades. At schools like DePauw, Albion, Illinois Wesleyan, Ohio Wesleyan, Grinnel, and Oberlin, future pastors and lay leaders were encouraged to take seriously the lifelong vocation of peacemaking. The Fellowship of Reconciliation was the leading pacifist institution on the American scene. Other respected voices like missionaries Kirby Page and E. Stanley Jones and *Christian Century* editor Charles Clayton Morrison urged the church to follow the "way of Jesus," by which they meant total opposition to all war. Even Reinhold Niebuhr was an active leader in the Fellowship of Reconciliation and remained in the pacifist camp until the early 1930s when he abandoned his earlier position and, with the publication of *Moral Man and Immoral Society* in 1932, made it clear that he no longer believed nonviolence to be a viable political strategy in the pursuit of justice (Reinhold Niebuhr, *Moral Man and Immoral Society: A Study in Ethics and Politics* [New York: C. Scribner's Sons, 1932]). The list of prominent pastors and teachers who supported

a pacifist stance was long and impressive — that is, until the Second World War began.

4. Long, *Living the Discipline*, 66.

5. *The Book of Discipline of the United Methodist Church* (Nashville: United Methodist Publishing House, 2000), Article 16, ¶103, 71.

6. *The Book of Discipline of the United Methodist Church* (Nashville: United Methodist Publishing House, 1996), ¶69C, 104–5; ¶68G, 103 (emphasis added).

7. Long, *Living the Discipline*, 152.

8. Weber, *Politics in the Order of Salvation*, 465–66 n. 88.

9. Ibid., 387.

10. Ibid., 354–55, 386.

11. In recent years, the Presbyterian Church U.S.A. has been deeply involved in discussions such as these through its Presbyterian Peacemaking Program. See also the discussion of Reinhold Niebuhr, Just Peace, and the Presbyterian Church U.S.A. in Ronald Stone, "Christian Realism and Peacemaking," *Review and Expositor* 79 (Fall 1982): 639–50. Similarly, the Lutheran Church–Missouri Synod found itself divided during both world wars and during the Vietnam War between those relying on traditional just-war doctrine and those taking up pacifism. See Jon Pahl, *Hopes and Dreams of All: The International Walther League and Lutheran Youth in American Culture, 1893–1993* (Chicago: Wheat Ridge Ministries, 1993), 261–80.

12. Aristotle, *Nicomachean Ethics*, trans. David Ross (Oxford: Oxford University Press, 1925), 35.

13. "A Social Statement on For Peace in God's World," available online from wwwtest.elca.org/dcs/peacein.html; accessed March 28, 2003.

14. Mark Hanson, "Statement in Response to U.S. Pre-emptive Military Strike against Iraq," available from wwwtest.elca.org/bishop/iraq_031903.html; accessed March 23, 2003.

15. Paul Ramsey and Stanley Hauerwas, *Speak Up for Just War or Pacifism* (University Park: Pennsylvania State University Press, 1988).

16. See, for example, Glen Stassen, *Just Peacemaking: Transforming Initiatives for Justice and Peace* (Louisville: Westminster/John Knox, 1992); Glen Stassen, ed., *Just Peacemaking: Ten Practices for Abolishing War* (Cleveland: Pilgrim Press, 1998); or C. Dale White, *Making a Just Peace: Human Rights and Domination Systems* (Nashville: Abingdon, 1998). The just-peace tradition is both a more "modern assessment" and rooted in ancient commitments to nonviolence. This view suggests that a Christian's calling is to be a committed peacemaker day after day, year after year, remembering that Jesus blessed the peacemakers. Just-peace principles include such concepts as:

- *Peacemaking is a sacred calling* of the gospel, blessed by God, making us evangelists of shalom–peace that is overflowing with justice, compassion, and well-being.

- *Government is a natural institution* of human community in God's creation and a requirement for the restraint of human evil. Every policy of government must be an act of justice and must be measured by its impact on the poor, the weak, and the oppressed.

- The *transformation* of the conflict-ridden nation-state system into a new world order of common security in interdependent institutions such as the United Nations *offers the only practical hope for enduring peace.*

- *Security is not only a legitimate concern* but an imperative responsibility of governments for the protection of life and well-being.

- *All Christians* — pacifists and nonpacifists — ought to *share a strong moral presumption against violence, killing, and warfare,* seeking every possible means of peaceful conflict resolution. The gospel command to love enemies is more than a benevolent ideal. It is essential to our well-being and survival.

- *Peacemaking* in the nuclear age, under the sovereignty of the Creator God, *requires the defense of creation* itself against possible assaults that may be rationalized in the name of national defense.

- The *church of Jesus Christ,* in the power and unity of the Holy Spirit, is *called to serve as an alternative community* to an alienated and fractured world. It is therefore to be a loving and peaceable international company of disciples transcending all governments, races, and ideologies; reaching out to all enemies; and ministering to all victims of poverty and oppression.

(These principles for just peace come from an unpublished letter by United Methodist Bishop C. Dale White, who served as one of the chief drafters of the 1988 *In Defense of Creation* Bishop's Pastoral Letter).

17. Weber, *Politics in the Order of Salvation,* 388.

18. Brad Kallenberg, *Ethics as Grammar: Changing the Postmodern Subject* (Notre Dame, Ind.: University of Notre Dame Press, 2001).

19. Ibid., 230.

20. Weber, *Politics in the Order of Salvation,* 373.

21. Ibid., 375.

22. See Kallenberg, *Ethics as Grammar,* 162–65.

23. Albert Outler, ed., *The Works of John Wesley,* vol. 1, *Sermons I:1–33* (Nashville: Abingdon, 1984), 517–18 (emphasis added).

24. Ronald Rolheiser, *The Holy Longing: The Search for a Christian Spirituality* (New York: Doubleday, 1998), 45–70.

25. Ibid., 53ff.

26. These notions of the essential role that the practices of Eucharist and Baptism may play in the pursuit of justice come from private correspondence between Amerson and Sample during the summer of 2002. Sample writes that he is currently doing a series of lectures arguing that a Christian stance of justice is most compelling when based on the Eucharist.

27. Robert McAfee Brown, *Creative Dislocation — The Movement of Grace* (Nashville: Abingdon, 1988), 18.

28. Alan Jones, *Sacrifice and Delight: Spirituality for Ministry* (San Francisco: HarperCollins, 1992), 94.

29. William T. Cavanaugh, *Torture and Eucharist: Theology, Politics and the Body of Christ* (Oxford: Blackwell Publishers, 1998).

# CHAPTER TWO

# PRAYER PRACTICES
# FOR THE WAY OF PEACE

*Andrew Dreitcer*

*Prayer is not so much formally addressing God with a list of requests as it is acknowledging that our connection to God is absolute, and unending, and urgent.*[1]

Recently, as I was marching with tens of thousands of others to protest the war in Iraq, I was forced to face what it means for me to be a person of peace, a bearer of peace, a builder of peace. My reflections evoked two memories, from the street and from the monastery.

## A MEMORY FROM THE STREET

A little over twenty years ago, the U.S. military buildup of the 1980s was beginning to impact the national psyche. A seminary student at the time, I joined with a group of other students who were training to engage in civil disobedience and nonviolent resistance as a protest against tax dollars being withdrawn from services for the poor and directed to the production of weapons. Specifically, we were planning to take part in a large protest at the gates of a nearby shipyard that built nuclear attack submarines. One submarine in production at the time had been "christened" the *Corpus Christi;*[2] we were horrified that a machine designed for devastating destruction might carry out its mission under the name of the one we called the Prince of Peace.

At the shipyard, events unfolded as planned. Crowds filled the streets carrying placards and signs. Chants for peace rang out almost without ceasing. My professor, Henri Nouwen, led us in a powerful liturgy. Our careful attempts to be respectful of the police and of their responsibilities bore fruit in the orderly arrest of about a dozen of my friends.

But as my companions were being helped into police vans and as the meditative chants we had been singing took on a distinctly triumphalistic tone and rhythm of militaristic fervor, I grew uneasy. I glanced at Henri Nouwen, hoping to find reassurance in his face. Here was a man whom millions viewed as a guide for the spiritual life. I trusted him to calm my growing dis-ease. Instead, in his face I found only anxiety — or was it anguish? In any case, I did not find there the calm and assurance I sought. Next I looked beyond the fence, to the inside of the shipyard where workers had begun to gather. There I saw fury. We were calling for the shipyard's military contracts to end. What would that mean for these workers' jobs, for their livelihoods, for their families?

I had been calling this a peaceful protest, an action for peace, but where now was the peace of God? Here were destructive anger, anxiety, anguish, dis-ease — none of which seemed to me to speak of the "peace that passes understanding." What was I to make of peace in this context?

## A MEMORY FROM THE MONASTERY

Just months before the protest at the shipyard, I had returned from a year-long stay at the French community of Taizé. Taizé is a sixty-year-old ecumenical Christian monastic community comprising more than a hundred men from all over the world. In a tiny medieval village in Burgundy, the brothers live a life of contemplation and action committed to reconciliation between the faiths and peoples of the world. Their thrice-daily "common prayers" bring together elements of the Roman Catholic, Protestant, and Eastern Orthodox churches in a beautiful liturgy of scripture, hymns, sung Psalms, darkness, icons, candles, and meditative chants written by and for the community. At the heart of these common prayers is an extended period of silence. In these moments of silence, the brothers wordlessly wait on God, attend to God's presence, together. In fact, this time of contemplative stillness forms the nourishing center of the community's life with God.

I went to Taizé on a spiritual quest, wanting to immerse myself in a life that would form me more fully in the ways of faith. I went to help the brothers welcome and care for the thousands of young people that visit the community each week. Once there, though, I struggled mightily. All the characteristics that I had embraced as defining my very being were of little value in the life I encountered at Taizé. My academic accomplishments, the people I knew, my knowledge of theology, and the impressive places I had studied seemed inconsequential. My life in community consisted not of the theological study I adored, but of kitchen chores, scrubbing bathrooms, cleaning the silent retreat house, building fences, and trying to maintain some semblance of order among the thousands of young backpackers who showed up daily to camp in the fields around the village. Thankfully, woven through the drudgery were the common prayers; three times a day they offered me an escape.

After several months I had almost exhausted my tolerance with this way of life. I determined to tell my sorrows to my spiritual director, Brother Thomas, with whom I met weekly. My litany of anxiety, anguish, anger, and dis-ease ended with, "I really don't like my life here. Nothing seems fulfilling to me. I'm having a very hard time. In fact, all I like is the common prayers. If it weren't for the prayers I wouldn't even be here!" Brother Thomas looked at me for a long time, an uncomfortably long time. Finally, he said, "If it weren't for the prayers you wouldn't be here? *Well, none of us would be!*"

The prayers were the heart and soul of the thing. The prayers were meant to flow in and through and around their entire lives, transforming each part of them, filling even mundane chores with the spirit of prayer. They trusted that over the long haul, the prayers would transform destructive anxiety, anguish, anger, and dis-ease into God's peace. Without their prayers, they could not practice the peace of God.

Truly I believe what Brother Thomas showed me. His way, carried in my memory of the monastery, is the way of the great Christian spiritual leaders. This way, I trust, counteracts the dis-ease that fills that other memory I harbor, the "memory of the street." In the face of a sense of poisonous, destructive confusion, prayer offers me an antidote. To speak of prayer as an "antidote" may seem odd at first blush. But many early Christians viewed prayer as the peacebearing curative for what they understood to be diseases of the soul. For instance, Evagrius of Pontus (c. 345–99) believed that prayer healed the soul, restoring it to its original divine image of calm.[3] Of course, such notions of prayer carried with them entire cosmologies, theologies, and anthropologies that may strike our twenty-first-century sensibilities as foreign, even bizarre.[4] At the very least, we ought not to assume we can easily understand such ancient concepts. What, for example, did Evagrius mean by "original divine image"?

Answering such questions, in all their complexities, is beyond the scope of this chapter. Still, I want to suggest that in the ancients' words and lives we can find certain enduring truths about the human psyche, spirit, and condition. This is especially the case, I believe, in ancient Christian views of the peacebearing role of prayer. So, in this chapter I draw extensively on early Christian wisdom as I discuss the nature and practice of prayer in relation to the building of peace in ourselves and in the world. First, I explore the notion of interior peace. Then I offer suggestions about the nature of prayer in our contemporary context. Finally, I describe ways of praying, as well as the historical and conceptual contexts from which they have arisen.

## INTERIOR PEACE

The earliest Christians insisted that becoming a person of prayer fosters a life of peace that came to be referred to as "detachment." The apostle Paul paved the way for this notion in its Christian form when he taught the faithful to "pray without ceasing" as they sought lives that were "in this world, but not of this world" (1 Thess. 5:17). Over the ages the notion of detachment has been much misunderstood and often misused. Many have taken it to mean a state of uncaring retreat from responsibility, an ignoring of calls to live in active love. In fact, those who have sought true lives of detachment view it quite differently.

Beginning in the fourth century the notion of what I call "practicing the peace of God" appears with particular strength among the desert monastics of Egypt, Palestine, and Syria. The desert sages went into the wilderness to "be solitary, be silent, and be at peace."[5] We have no extensive written descriptions of the details, shape, and texture of the experience of inner peace the sages sought. Still, some of the writings refer to the "single eye" of life directed toward God; attention of the heart to God; and "the all-wise knowledge of God," which is "the crown of the virtues." All of these attributes of the spiritual life are connected to a heart of stability and peace.[6] Further, the monks speak of "stillness" (*hesuchian* — "hesychasm"), a sense of "inner tranquility and silence."[7] This is a profound "quiet, the calm through the whole [person] that is like a still pool of water, capable of reflecting the sun. To be in true relationship with God, standing before [God] in every situation — that was the angelic life, the spiritual life, the monastic life, the aim and the way of the monk."[8] With this inner quiet came *apatheia*, the experience of inner freedom, freedom from anxious caring. This was a state of feeling dependent only on God. In this state the sages enjoyed "detachment," freedom from "inordinate attachments." This was not a state of cold, distant uncaring. Instead, it was a sense of "freedom from anxiety about the future; freedom from the tyranny of haunting memories of the past; freedom from an attachment to the ego which precluded intimacy with others and God."[9] Today, we might say that they sought lives free of addictions, both large and small. They sought to allow the Spirit of God to flow through their lives unimpeded.

In the ages following the desert monastics, even the most thorough-going mystics, those who may seem the most intent on being "not of this world," have insisted that the purpose of the Christian life is actively to love one another. Most accurately, then, detachment has referred to a steadiness, a stability, at the core of one's being. In this state (the pure form of which is seldom, if ever, experienced), the center of the self is firmly anchored in or attached to God. Because of this stable grounding, one is able to be open to whatever may come in life. One is able to receive and appropriately respond to the gravest threat or to the most wondrous joy. Detachment, then, speaks of a grounded interior openness, an interior readiness, a lack of obsessions, a lack of addictions, an ability to attend to the Christian call to act with love in the world.

In other words, to speak of detachment is to speak of a state of interior peace. Such a grounded peace expands beyond the interior life into one's interpersonal relationships, one's relationship with the environment, and one's interactions with the systems and structures of the world. The soul at peace bears peace to others, builds a just peace in the world. From a place of interior peace, we can act appropriately, justly, mercifully, with legitimate anger that is not simply the external expression of our own unresolved wounds, issues, anxieties, and fears. For this stillness, this peace, does not foster a passive presence in the world. Quite the contrary: this is the place of fearlessness, from which a grounded courage comes, a clarity of purpose, a compassion of heart that refuses to trample human lives and the gift of creation just as surely as it refuses to allow lives and creation to be trampled.

## THE NATURE OF CHRISTIAN PRAYER[10]

Stillness of soul, interior peace, is not easy to achieve. In fact, most, if not all, strands of the Christian tradition insist that interior peace can

*never* be *achieved;* it is a divine gift. And yet, the traditions insist that
in some mysterious way the gift of peace most easily finds its resting
place in the soul that is nurtured by prayer. Perhaps it is fair to say that
though prayer is *not necessary* for bringing interior peace, its presence
is *inevitable* in the lives of those who discover this holy gift.[11]

Of course prayer itself, as the struggles of Christian sages have demonstrated over the centuries, is no easy thing. The desert monastics,
after all, experienced prayer as a foreign battleground for the soul's
struggle to fullness of life. Robert McAfee Brown suggests a similar
idea, though with a less militaristic metaphor:

> Prayer for many is like a foreign land. When we go there, we go
> as tourists. Like most tourists, we feel uncomfortable and out of
> place. Like most tourists, we therefore move on before too long
> and go somewhere else.[12]

How do we enter into this foreign land? How can we settle there?
Surely God's grace invites us to go and offers us the courage to remain.
But how can we respond to God's desire for us? What is the process of
becoming a person of prayer?

In offering an answer to these questions, I want to give here a taste
of some of the ways the tradition of Christian prayer may help us grow
our souls into prayerful containers of stillness, dwelling places for the
peace of God. Before turning to explore some of the many ways of
prayer available to us, it may be important to say a bit about what I
mean by prayer.

Christian history offers no uniform definition for any of the classical terms describing prayer. Even when Christian writers use the
same terms to describe the same movement or moment or disposition or aspect of prayer, they may conceptualize in very different
ways what they are meaning by the term. For instance, scholars of
early- and late-medieval Christianity point out that we cannot take the
word "contemplation" at face value in any writing, because a seventh-
century writer will be thinking of it in a way that differs appreciably

from the way a fourteenth-century writer conceives of it — even when they seem to be writing of the same moment in prayer. The earlier writer might be describing a form of contemplation that consists of the mind carefully considering concepts concerned with the nature of God, while the latter might be speaking of being absorbed in an affective sense of love for God. The theological and philosophical systems connected with their experiences and the personal and social contexts in which they live form their prayer experiences in significantly different ways.

Perhaps the best place to begin in trying to encompass the breadth of experiences of Christian prayer is to consider the ancient tradition of *lectio divina* ("holy reading"). It seems that the practice of *lectio divina* began developing prior to the fifth century among desert monastics, though an expanded, formalized description of *lectio divina* does not appear until the twelfth century. In *The Ladder of Monks,* Guigo II (d. 1188?) specifies four "rungs" in the process, by which monks "are lifted up to heaven":

> ...reading [*lectio*], meditation [*meditatio*], prayer [*oratio,* or prayerful expressions directed to God], and contemplation [*contemplatio*]...Reading [the Bible and other spiritually helpful books], as it were puts food whole into the mouth, meditation chews it and breaks it up, prayer extracts its flavor, contemplation is the sweetness itself which gladdens and refreshes.[13]

Other twelfth-century writers compare the practice of *lectio divina* to a cow with her cud: pray-ers "ruminate" on what they read, speaking (mouthing) it to themselves over and over, deriving nourishment from it as they "chew" it, "swallow" it into memory, and later "belch" it up to ruminate on it again.[14] The pray-ers trust that they become what they "eat." Praying, they believe, transforms them inside and out into a living Word of God.

Arguably, each form of Christian prayer practice that has developed over the ages can be found within the movements of *lectio divina*. These ancient movements show us that prayer's process of moving us into a grounding stillness of the soul may take many forms: focusing our attention and opening ourselves in preparation (as attentive reading and *ruminatio* do); studied consideration of an idea, object, sensory experience, or affective experience (experienced in *meditatio*); expressing to God our hopes, our fears, our joys, our longings, our thanksgivings, our angers, our deepest selves (the essence of *oratio*); or simply soaking in the presence of God in whatever way that comes to us (*contemplatio*[15]). Not surprisingly, each of the Christian traditions has tended to emphasize particular movements within *lectio divina*. In the Protestant tradition, for instance, *oratio* has dominated, while other traditions, such as the Eastern Orthodox churches, have more fully emphasized *contemplatio*.

As we engage these varieties of prayer, certain questions may arise: What does praying have to do with God? Who or what is this God? What kind of God is implied by the practice of prayer?

Though I am not writing a theological treatise, it may be helpful to present some basic assumptions about God that are connected to my own practice and understanding of prayer. I offer these not as prescriptions. Rather, I hope that my own transparency sparks you to consider more deeply your own understandings of the relationship between prayer and the Divine Presence you know.

Briefly, "God" is the word that names for me the endlessly creative source of love, justice, compassion, hope, and peace that pervades the universe. Within this broad definition, I offer five theological assumptions that I have drawn from what I see as the heart of Christianity: intimacy, sovereign ubiquity, variety, mystery, and longing.

1. *Intimacy.* The God of my experience, the God I see portrayed in scripture through Jesus of Nazareth, the God whose presence I look to encounter in every moment through the Holy Spirit, is an intimate God, a God of loving intimacy. God is more than personal. God is suprapersonal.[16] God is closer to us than we are to ourselves;

so close to us that we often miss God's presence with us; so close that we often miss the Christ in us and in the people we know and meet; so close that we often miss the presence of the Spirit in the world around us. God is that immanent, that intimate. In God "we live and move and have our being" (Acts 17:28).

2. *Sovereign ubiquity.* For me, God's nature includes awesome omnipresence, being present with and in and over and under and through all time and space, everywhere, in all things — and greater than and beyond all things, too. God comes to us in every part of life: through scripture, within ourselves, through other people, in our connections with the social systems in which we work and live and play, in our experience of nature and the environment in which we live, and in written and artistic and other expressions of culture. In each of these parts of life God is waiting for us. I assume that if we begin to look at life with new eyes, with a certain attentiveness, with a certain expectation, we can begin to catch glimpses of the holy. We will sense the activity of something that just might be the ripples of the presence of God.

3. *Variety.* God comes to us in a variety of ways, according to the gifts, struggles, capacities, contexts, genetic heritage, and personalities unique to each of our lives. Divine Presence accommodates itself to the quirks of each individual and each community. The Bible is full of stories that vividly illustrate this, from Noah to Ruth, Nicodemus to Thomas, Martha and beyond.

4. *Mystery.* Even God's intimacy is part of the vastly mysterious nature of God, the infinite transcendence of God. To put this in the form of a question: How can such a vast mystery be so intimately known by us? Or put another way: God is immanent in a way that is transcendent, in a way that goes beyond our understanding, that is utterly mysterious.[17] Even God's intimacy with us is a mysterious thing.

5. *Longing.* God is a God who longs for us. This mysterious, sovereign, intimate, ubiquitous God of Jesus longs for us, calls to us, beckons to us, invites us. And in that longing, God attracts, and summons, and calls forth from us (and all creation) something new. This God keeps drawing us in a spiritual direction, attracting us by the sheer power of pure love, pure grace. And so God's longing activity, or God's activity of longing, works on us to heal our wounds, to free us from sin, to animate us toward lovingly transforming the world for justice and peace, to fill us with new life, to finally reconcile all things in God.

What role, then, does prayer play in relation to such a Presence, a God of intimacy, sovereign ubiquity, variety, mystery, and longing? I suggest that this God welcomes and creatively embraces whatever we have to offer, whatever expression of ourselves, our lives, our world brews and bubbles up from within our selves and our communities. In this way, at least, prayer "works": those who pray are changed.[18] Arguably, every strand of the Christian tradition stresses that prayer is primarily a divine gift for those who pray. Prayer is not meant as a tool for manipulating God or the world. Ultimately, whatever its form, Christian prayer is a process of developing intimacy with God through *intentionally communing with Divine Presence*. It is in intimately communing with God that we find the place of grounded stillness of soul. In the gift of intimately communing with Divine Presence we enter more fully into the life of God as we experience more of God's fullness in, through, with, around, and among us. In prayer we come more fully to practice the peace of God.

## WAYS OF PRAYING

As I have suggested, the Christian tradition has developed a richness of prayer. There may be a form of prayer for every sensibility. In this section I present a number of ways of praying that may be practiced in order to help form an interior foundation for peace in oneself and in the world.

### The Prayer of Preparation: "Recollection"

Often our prayers can be thwarted by distractions from within ourselves and from beyond ourselves. The Christian tradition is keenly aware of this problem, and early on developed ways of addressing it — as the specific movements of reading and ruminating in *lectio divina* suggest. A more generalized approach to the process of preparing ourselves for prayer is seen in the practice of "recollection." "Recollection" refers to a process in which our attention is drawn into ourselves so that we are focused on God and on our presence before God.

Some of the classical descriptions of this practice are found in the writings of Teresa of Avila.[19] She uses several images to describe recollection. In the first one she describes a person, the soul, as being like a castle. At the center of the castle is the Sovereign, God. The people of the castle are all the human senses and faculties or abilities (e.g., feeling, thinking, hearing, understanding, willing). Much of the time, these people, these abilities or faculties, are wandering around busy outside the castle. But at points they gather into the castle, they become collected within the castle, focused together on being with the Sovereign and at the service of the Sovereign. All our energies, rather than being scattered to various attentions, are now focused on one thing — the thing at the heart of it all, God. Teresa also describes this process as being like a turtle drawing into its shell, or like a hedgehog curling up, drawing into itself in stillness.[20]

Throughout the Christian tradition, recollection can be found referring both to a *state* that is simply *given by God* and to some *action intentionally taken by the pray-er* to gather himself or herself in order to be open to and focused on God. In either case, the effect on the pray-er is the same: a movement toward a sense of stillness, collectedness, composedness, centeredness, in the presence of God, focused on God.

One contemporary writer notes that the word "recollection" has at least two illuminating connotations: (1) re-collecting ourselves — bringing the movements and parts and functions of ourselves into some semblance of order and focus; (2) remembering — remembering who and what lies beneath and within and around our lives, and remembering to stop living without attention to God and to remember to live with attention on God.[21]

The practice of recollection may, of course, serve as a prayer in its own right; in it we are gathering ourselves into a time of communing with God. As I have suggested, though, this practice can be helpful as a prelude to other ways of praying. With that in mind, I offer a simple exercise of preparation, a prayer of recollection that may precede whatever prayer you feel led to.

## Recollection

1. Find a place and time that is free (as free as possible, that is) of external distractions. You may wish to have a lighted candle, a favorite religious image, flowers, or some other object that evokes for you the sense that you are devoting this time and place to your life with God.

2. Settle yourself into a comfortable position, one that allows for ease of breathing, one that does not constrict any part of your body.

3. Allow yourself to relax by engaging in one or more of the following:

   a. Playing gentle or meditative music.

   b. Reading a favorite passage of scripture or some other favorite spiritual writing.

   c. Singing a song or meditative chant that you know will calm you.

   d. Focus on relaxing the muscles in every part of your body: First let the muscles in your head and face soften. Slowly and gradually, one bit at a time, relax the muscle regions throughout your body, all the way to your toes.

e. Notice your breathing, and count your breaths from one to ten and back to one again.

4. In whatever way is appropriate for you, ask for or acknowledge God's gracious presence with you in this time and in the prayer you are about to engage.

### The Prayer of Desire

Christian pray-ers throughout the ages have insisted that prayer begins with desire, with longing. According to Ann and Barry Ulanov, "We long for contact, for connection at the center, that grounding that brings full-hearted peace of mind and soul. We want to be in touch with what lives within every thing that matters, with what truly satisfies."[22] Even though our longing for God "hides in lesser desires,"[23] it is our yearning for the Divine that turns us to seek a sense of God's peace in our lives. It is our desire for God that fuels our search to build God's peace in the world.

The Psalmist expresses this yearning again and again:

> Hear, O Lord, when I cry aloud,
>   be gracious to me and answer me!
> "Come," my heart says, "seek [God's] face!"
>   Your face, O Lord, do I seek.
> Do not hide your face from me. (Ps. 27:7–9)

> As a deer longs for flowing streams,
>   so my soul longs for you, O God. (Ps. 42:1)

### Three Prayer Practices around Desire

The following three prayer practices are meant to help us know ourselves in relation to God. Throughout Christian history the process of knowing self has been inseparably linked to knowing God. John Calvin, for instance, puts it this way in the opening section of his *Institutes of the Christian Religion:* "Without knowledge of self there is no knowledge of God.... [T]he knowledge of ourselves not only arouses us to seek God, but as it were, leads us by the hand to find him."[24]

It is important to recall that in the dominant understanding of "knowing," God is not limited to intellectual understanding, knowing *about* God. Instead, "knowing" carries the meaning of "multifaceted experience" or, as one scholar puts it, "existential apprehension."[25] Such knowledge is similar to the way the Hebrew Bible employs "knowing" as a term for sexual union.

In the case of the three prayer practices below, the part of the self we are coming to know is our desire for God. The Christian spiritual tradition insists that as we identify our deepest longing (perhaps a longing for peace), we will be led toward God, for we will follow the desire we uncover. In other words, our desire nurtures in us a growing sense of God's deep and expansive intimacy in our lives. There, in the midst of this expanding intimacy, is the place where the still and powerful peace of God dwells with us.

1. *Lectio Divina I: Engaging Words*

   a. Prepare to read Mark 10:46–51a.

   b. "Recollect" yourself (see "The Prayer of Preparation" above).

   c. Slowly read the passage several times (preferably aloud at least once), ending with the phrase, "What do you want me to do for you?"

   d. Repeat this question to yourself again and again. That is, ruminate on it, chewing it over and over until the question seems to be asking itself. Perhaps this rumination will last for minutes. Perhaps it will linger for days.

   e. At some point in your rumination, you may sense an urge to respond. Follow that urge. Speak or write the desire that comes to you.

f. Conclude with a prayer that expresses to God what has arisen for you in this time.

2. *Lectio Divina II: Engaging the Imagination*

While the prayer above may be accessible to those who easily and fruitfully engage word-formed ideas, this prayer may be more accessible to those for whom the imagination holds particular power. Central to this kind of prayer, which is especially associated with Ignatius of Loyola in the sixteenth century, is the ancient belief that God inspires our imaginations through the stories of the Bible. According to this tradition, the richness of a scripture-inspired imagination offers a fertile context for revealing our deepest selves in communion with Divine Presence.

a. Prepare to read Mark 10:46–51a.

b. "Recollect" yourself (see "The Prayer of Preparation" above).

c. Slowly read the passage twice, ending with the phrase, "What do you want me to do for you?"

d. Set the passage aside and begin to review in your memory what you have read: the people, the place, the actions, the conversations. As you review these elements of the passage, let your imagination begin to construct the scene they form. (Do not worry about getting the scene "right." In this way of praying, scripture inspires a richness of images that exceeds the written details.) What do you see? Hear? Smell? Feel? Whom do you see? What colors are visible? What buildings and vegetation? What do you notice about Jesus? As the scene unfolds, imagine that he ultimately turns to you with the question, "What do you want me to do for you?" Hear that question again and again. Notice how Jesus asks it — the way he looks and sounds.

e. Begin to answer Jesus' question. You may wish to carry on a conversation with him, either imagining it within you or writing it out as a dialogue.

f. Conclude with a prayer that expresses to God what has arisen for you in this time.

3. *A Prayer of Noticing*

a. At the beginning of the day, pose these questions to yourself: "What does desire look like in my life?" "What does desire *for* God look like in my life?"

b. Invite God to draw your attention to your desire as you go through your day.

c. Throughout the day, where do you notice desire appearing? Is it desire for God? If so, what keeps this desire for God contained? Where do you imagine it is headed?

d. At the end of the day, recall what you noticed and offer a prayer that expresses to God what has arisen for you in this time.

## Prayers of Attentiveness

### Self-Examination: Giving and Receiving Peace

Since the first few centuries of Christianity, Christians have practiced a form of prayer in which they examine their behaviors and their interior experiences in relation to the world around them. For instance, the early desert monastics regularly reported all their thoughts and actions to an *abba* or *amma* (a wise spiritual "father" or "mother"). In the sixteenth century, Ignatius of Loyola developed what is known as the "awareness examen," a prayerful review of one's daily actions, concerns, thoughts, and feelings. Similarly, the Puritans and Protestants engaged in "examination of the conscience" or "examination of consciousness" through journaling, prayerful consideration, or conversing with a trusted spiritual guide. Those who practice these and other forms of self-examination trust that such focused attention helps them live ever more fully the way of God's love in their lives. The prayer practice below offers a taste of this tradition with particular attention to the experience of peace.

Throughout the day:

Pay attention to the people, events, and circumstances around you.

Notice how you are responding to . . .

- The people you meet
- Your physical surroundings (the natural world, the room you are in, etc.)
- The rhythms and structures and patterns of the day
- The situations you find yourself in
- The thoughts and feelings that arise in you

Questions to keep gently before you:

Where am I receiving a sense of peace? Where am I not receiving a sense of peace?

Where am I offering the way of peace or helping build peace?

Where am I not offering the way of peace or not helping build peace?

At the end of the day:

1. Offer yourself to God's caring presence — as you allow your mind and body to quiet.

2. Ask to be shown what the Spirit wants you to receive — to see, feel, and understand.

3. Look back slowly over the events, persons, circumstances of the day. Ask yourself, "When did I *least* experience peace being given, formed, or received?"

In response to this question, allow your awareness to settle on one piece of the day that particularly draws your attention. What feelings were connected with that person, event, circumstance (joy, pain, turmoil, increased sense of love, anger, harmony, anxiety, freedom, etc.)? Ask yourself why these feelings arose. What awareness does this bring to you about your life? — about your life with God? How was God present to you in that time?

4. Write in your journal.

5. Repeat steps 1–4, above, but this time using the question, "When did I *most* fully experience peace being given or received?"

6. In light of your experience in this prayer, do you have any sense of being called or invited to effect deeper transformation — in yourself and/or in the world? What might that be?

7. Offer a prayer in response to what has come to you in this time.

## Praying with Creation

In exploring the spiritual lives of many individuals and communities over the years, I have noticed how important the created world is for the spiritual life. More people describe to me encounters with God (as they define God) through experiences of and in nature — the forest, a garden, the ocean, the mountains, storms — than through experience of any other type. Activities such as reading scripture, worshiping, listening to sermons, being with friends and loved ones, studying, and music are not mentioned as often as being in nature. This is true across the theological spectrum. Further, descriptions of the spiritual power of communing with nature appear in Christian writings throughout the ages.

1. Go to a place where God's creation meets you. Ask for God's presence with you.

2. Attend to the works of creation around you. Does one thing seem to invite you, strike you, impress you, or somehow attract you?

3. Come to a sense of focused attention in the presence of God and this piece of God's handiwork.

4. Simply gaze upon this part of creation for an extended time — a time of wonder, amazement, openness, receiving.

5. Eventually, engage God in conversation about this thing you have noticed. You may want to ask God questions such as: Where has it been? Who has seen, touched, held, experienced it? Why does God value it? How is it related to what is around it? How is it related to me? — to the rest of creation? What does it tell me of myself?

6. Consider these questions: How do I experience God present to me through this piece of creation? What have I learned of God through it? What have I been offered? What have I received? In what way is peace a part of what I am being offered — or not?

7. Remain for a time in the experience of whatever follows these questions.

8. Offer God thanks for this time and for the wonders of creation.

## Attending to "Thoughts"

The ancient desert tradition practiced attention to what the monastics referred to as "thoughts" (*logismoi*) — interior movements that arise unbidden within a person. These thoughts included what we might now call near-obsessive feelings, images, emotions, ideas, and imaginings. The desert sages believed that the thoughts functioned as inclinations that moved them toward particular behaviors. All too easily the thoughts can take over a life, moving through obsessions to addictions. If responded to with proper attention — prayer, spiritual disciplines, and the help of a spiritual guide — the impact of the thoughts in a life offers an opportunity for discerning and bettering the state of the soul's communion with God. In short, how one responds to the thoughts helps determine the path ahead. Some responses lead to active distraction from God's way. Others help the monastic live more fully into life with God.

The following prayer practice gives contemporary expression to the ancient notion of attending to one's thoughts or inclinations. This version of the prayer focuses on behaviors and thoughts that may or may not build peace.

1. Turn your attention to the different behaviors in your life during the past week. How do you spend your time? How do you treat the people you know? How do you respond to people you meet in passing? What are your routines of work and leisure?

2. Are there particular behaviors that seem harmful to you or others, that create an environment that works against peace in yourself, in others, and/or in the world?

3. Consider the thoughts and inclinations that arise regularly within you. What connection do you notice between these and the harmful behaviors you have identified? Is there a particular thought or inclination that directs you off track?

4. Experiment with praying in the following way (every day, if possible).

   a. Identify a short prayer (perhaps a phrase from a Psalm) that you sense somehow draws you more fully along God's path of peace. (The desert sages first used Psalm 70:1 or Psalm 40:13 as their prayer — "O God make speed to save me: O Lord make haste to help me.")

   b. When the unhelpful thought/inclination comes up (this could be many times a day!), notice it and name it to yourself. ("I've snapped at my daughter — *again*.")

c. After naming it, begin to pray the short prayer you have identified as somehow helpful for you on your path with God (item
"a" above).

5. Note what, if anything, is happening within you in response to your
prayer.

### Prayers of Intention

Prayers of intention are about *being there,* being available. The heart
of such a prayer is this recognition: "I want to place myself in God's
presence." With this recognition, then, comes a practice conveyed by
these words: "I am placing myself in God's presence." Prayers of intention agree with the saying, "Most of life is just showing up." Or, as
Herb Hamrol, a hundred-year-old grocery store clerk in San Francisco,
puts it, "You stop showing up for things, you start falling apart."[26] Since
prayers of attention aim for nothing more than being there, they are,
perhaps, the simplest form of Christian prayer. This does not mean they
are easy. In fact, because most of us are trained to want to attain some
designated goal or accomplish some assigned task, prayers of intention
may be the most difficult to practice. They remind us that God is in our
lives for the long haul, and that the fruits of prayer may arise only over
time. These prayers do not offer instant gratification. No insights are
expected. No feelings are looked for. No images are hoped for. There is
only the basic intention defined by, "Now I am here, God." Those who
practice these prayers find that only gradually, in indiscernible increments, do they experience a growing sense of being attuned to God's
way, God's peace.

### Centering Prayer

Over the past thirty years a form of intention-prayer has developed
that is rooted in three traditional forms of Christian prayer: *lectio divina;*
the way of praying described in the anonymously written, fourteenth-
century work *The Cloud of Unknowing;* and "prayer of the heart" from

the early desert tradition.[27] Centering prayer draws from each of these traditions an emphasis on encountering God's presence in a way that does not depend on words, images, emotions, kinesthetic sensations, or other physical, conceptual, and affective experiences. Centering prayer depends on offering oneself to God's love. The author of *The Cloud of Unknowing*, for instance, describes a form of prayer in which the pray-er is immersed in an absence of thoughts, feelings, and sensations — a "cloud" in which previous ways of knowing God are no longer operative. Only love remains. Similarly, in *lectio divina* the dimension of *contemplatio* consists simply of being available to God, soaking in God's presence without any other agenda. And finally, the desert tradition practiced a form of prayer that progressed from repeating words with the mouth ("prayer of the body") to internally repeated "prayers of the mind" to a "prayer of the heart" (or "prayer of the mind in the heart").[28] In prayer of the heart, the praying is completely internalized. It continues without ceasing and with no effort from the pray-er. From prayer of the heart, the centering prayer tradition especially draws the notion of a deep communion with God that occurs beneath the pray-er's awareness.

Here is a simple form of centering prayer.

1. Settle yourself into a comfortable position that allows you to be peaceful and alert.

2. Attend to these words: "Now I am here. You are here. We are here." Repeat them a few times as a way of focusing your attention on the time at hand.

3. As you continue in silence for a few moments, consider this: "What word speaks to me of Divine Presence? What word draws me to be with God?" Let a word arise within you. This word will be your reminder that you are here now for God. (For some people the word might be *shalom* or love or freedom, or simply "here." If no word comes to you, you may wish to try one of these for a time.)

4. Set a timer for twenty minutes. (Most people who practice centering prayer do so for twenty minutes twice a day. You may want to begin with five minutes and work up.) During this time all you need to do is "be here" for God. That is your intention. When you notice you are no longer attuned to your intention, gently repeat your chosen word one or two times. The word serves to direct you back to your intention.

## Hourly Prayer

After my year at the monastery of Taizé, I sought a way of praying that would emulate in some way the thrice-daily common prayers of that community. For the Brothers (as for most monastics), over the years these daily "offices" became fundamentally prayers of intention, primarily a matter of showing up. As my life unfolded, I wished for a similar experience — especially in the midst of juggling two jobs and the wonders of family life. I ultimately settled on this simple way of praying (which depends on having the right kind of wristwatch):

Set your watch to chime on the hour.

When you hear the chime, focus on your intention to be with God. You might say to yourself, "Now I am here, God." Or you may repeat the word you use for centering prayer. Remain in this intention for one to five minutes.

For me, this simple prayer has offered a grounding sense of returning again and again to God's peace-filled presence in my life.

## Praying in the Heat of the Moment

For those of us who can manage to set aside a designated chunk of time each day for prayer, all the ways of praying I have described to this point may offer fruitful resources. But many of us have great difficulty finding and keeping such time. I share this problem. So, over the years, I have tended to gravitate toward prayers that I can practice on the run, along the way, in the heat of the moment. Two in particular continue to be important for me: "Kything" and the Jesus Prayer.

*Kything*

Madeline l'Engle coined the term "kything," deriving it from the Celtic phrase "kith and kin." For l'Engle, the word evokes a sense of relatedness or presence that — like the bonds of kith and kin — cannot be broken. Louis Savary and Patricia Berne have borrowed the term to describe a particular way of praying.[29] Kything prayer engages the imagination to focus on the interconnectedness between all people, all creatures, all creation, and God. It calls the pray-er to a stance of transformative love in relation to "the other." For many people, this form of prayer may be indispensable for building a truly just peace. I offer a version I have developed in my own life.

- Consider an individual or group that you are with or soon to be encountering. Hold them in your imagination.

- As you focus on them, imagine yourself being surrounded by a vital, God-filled light.

- Now imagine the other person or group being surrounded by a similar light.

- As your imagination holds both these images, allow the lights gradually to merge into one.

- Rest in this image for a time.

This prayer may be rather easily engaged when you are not in the heat of the encounter. But with a bit of practice, it is possible to be praying in this way even in the midst of a difficult meeting with people you may fear. In that case, the imagination carries on — caught up in the trust that within a single, divine light is room for the peace, justice, compassion, and creative love that flow from God.

## The Jesus Prayer

In the section on centering prayer, above, I discussed the desert tradition of "prayer of the heart." The Jesus Prayer represents a particularly defined form of this tradition. "Jesus Christ, Son of God, have mercy on me" is one version of the prayer, which has its roots in the biblical phrases "Jesus, Son of David, have mercy on me" (the blind man in Luke 18:38) and "God be merciful to me, a sinner" (the tax collector in the parable around Luke 18:13). As the monastic tradition in the Eastern church developed a sustained (centuries-long) practice of short, repetitious, biblically based prayers, the words of the Jesus Prayer (in a variety of versions) became the dominant prayer of this type. The prayer itself does not appear in any (extant) writings prior to the sixth century. It seems to retain the ancient Hebraic notion that there is divine power in speaking or meditating upon the divine name. One monk in the tradition describes the prayer in this way:

> [T]his prayer, when you have learnt to use it properly, or rather, when it becomes grafted to the heart, will lead you to the end which you desire: it will unite your mind with your heart, it will quell the turbulence of your thoughts, and it will give you power to govern the movements of your soul.[30]

For many years, I prayed my own version of this prayer: "Be with me, Jesus, in love and mercy." I recently returned to the traditional form. Whatever version you may embrace or create, those who practice such prayers say that their vitality comes through repetition, constant repetition. Eventually, it is said, as the prayer moves from the lips to the mind to the heart, it begins to "pray itself" continually, with no effort on the part of the pray-er. Thus, this kind of prayer can go on in the midst of work and play, stressful times and calm times, joys and sorrows. I have found that the slow, steady repetition does, indeed, ground the movements of my soul in the face of disruptive events and situations.

## A PRAYER FOR PEACE

I have been writing this chapter in my neighborhood bakery. Yesterday my friend Mike walked in for a sandwich, and I accepted his invitation to join him for lunch. Though Mike is Jewish in practice and in heritage, he regularly finds spiritual sustenance at the church where my wife is the pastor. As often happens, our conversation turned to matters of the soul. This day Mike spoke of a recent shift in his prayers. They had become more regular, more vital. To illustrate his point, he told of his recent competitive swim from Alcatraz Island to San Francisco. The strong San Francisco Bay winds hitting him from the left side and the force of the tide pushing him from the right side lifted the fifty-degree water into intimidating swells. As he struggled to maintain his course, his attention turned to prayer. And in that moment he experienced an incredible steadiness. He described it as a God-given "wave of calm." In the midst of the turbulence, Mike was set solidly on his path, facing the struggle without fear, at peace within himself.

I must admit that generally I am not fond of such transparent metaphors. But on this day I was particularly open to what Mike described. His story reminded me of the people I have met who seem to be steeped in a prayer-filled "wave of calm." I must confess that I am not one of those people. Yes, I know many ways of praying. But I know them because I am constantly seeking — not yet receiving — a sustained life of prayer. Especially at this time in my life, as my family struggles with the reality of my wife's recently diagnosed brain cancer, I yearn for the wave of calm that will allow me to fashion more fully a life of strength and hope, to build more completely a world of peace. Such a life includes protesting in the streets for just causes, finding ways of reconciling with difficult neighbors, and caring for loved ones who suffer the ravages of mortal bodies. Indeed, in such times I *have* occasionally *tasted* a deep, steadying calm. But I hunger for more, much more. So, full of that longing, I offer a simple prayer:

*May the peace which passes all understanding*
*fill our lives and our world. Amen.*

## NOTES

1. Melissa Tidwell, quoted in *Prayers for Courage: Words of Faith for Difficult Times* (Nashville: Upper Room, 2003), 31.

2. According to the Navy's description of its own conventions, the submarine had been named after a U.S. city — in this case, Corpus Christi, Texas. Knowing this fact did not diminish our fervor. Eventually (perhaps in response to protests around the country), the submarine was renamed "The City of Corpus Christi," a development that did little to mollify those of us who had joined in the original protests.

3. Teresa Shaw, *The Burden of the Flesh: Fasting and Sexuality in Early Christianity* (Minneapolis: Fortress Press, 1998), 159. In the ancients' words and lives can be found certain enduring truths about the human psyche, spirit, and condition. This is especially the case, I believe, in their views of the restorative role of prayer.

4. For a brilliant tour through the strange and wonderful conceptual world underlying early Christian spiritual practices, see Shaw, *The Burden of the Flesh.*

5. Abba Arsenius's rule for life.

6. *Lives of the Desert Fathers: The Historia Monachorum in Aegypto,* trans. Norman Russell, Introduction by Benedicta Ward (London: Mowbray, 1980), 97, 15, 31.

7. Ibid., 123 n. 8.

8. *The Sayings of the Desert Fathers: The Alphabetical Collection,* trans., Benedicta Ward (Kalamazoo, Mich.: Cistercian Publications, Inc., 1975), xxvi.

9. Douglas Burton-Christie, *The Word in the Desert: Scripture and the Quest for Holiness in Early Christian Monasticism* (Oxford: Oxford University Press, 1993), 214–22.

10. When I speak of prayer in this chapter, I am referring primarily to the practices of individuals at prayer. As much, if not more, could also be written on communal prayer and its relation to peace.

11. I thank my teacher and friend Eric Dean for introducing me almost thirty years ago to the notion of "not necessary, but inevitable." He touted it as the most accurate description of the Reformed Protestant notion of how sin arises in the individual person, but I have since seen it as applicable to many other mysteries of the divine-human relationship.

12. The source of this quote from Brown is unknown to me.

13. Guigo II, *"The Ladder of Monks: A Letter on the Contemplative Life"* and *"Twelve Meditations,"* trans. and with an introduction by Edmund Colledge and James Walsh (Kalamazoo, Mich.: Cistercian Publications, 1981), 68–69. Comments in brackets are mine. It is worth noting that the "texts" that may be "read" in this way include the natural world, one's own life, the lives of others, and the systems and social structures that pervade our world.

14. Michael Casey, "St. Benedict's Approach to Prayer," *Cistercian Studies* 15, no. 2 (1980): 337.

15. Generally in Eastern religions the term "meditation" refers to an experience akin to what the Christian tradition calls "contemplation."

16. David Kelsey offered me this notion — a life-transforming one for me — years ago in private conversation.

17. I draw this notion from William Placher's argument in *The Domestication of Transcendence: How Modern Thinking about God Went Wrong* (Louisville: Westminster John Knox, 1996).

18. I do not discount the possibility that prayer "works" in other ways as well. It makes sense to me to live in the hope that specific prayers are precisely answered. But I make no particular claims for such a cause-and-effect relationship; I hold too dear the limitations of human understanding and the mysterious natures of God and the universe.

19. *The Interior Castle,* described in the third chapter of the fourth Dwelling Place.

20. Francis de Sales quotes these last two images in his description of recollection in *The Love of God,* book 6, chapter 7.

21. Dwight H. Judy, *Embracing God: Praying with Teresa of Avila* (Nashville: Abingdon, 1996), 80.

22. Ann and Barry Ulanov, *Primary Speech: A Psychology of Prayer* (Atlanta: John Knox, 1982), 13.

23. Ibid.

24. John Calvin, *The Institutes of the Christian Religion,* ed. John T. McNeill, trans. Ford Lewis Battles (Philadelphia: Westminster Press, 1977), I,I,1.

25. For Lewis Battles's comment see ibid., I,I,1, n. 1.

26. Steve Rubenstein, "On the Job at 100 Years Old," *San Francisco Chronicle,* April 2, 2003, A-9.

27. Thomas Keating and John Main have been particularly important in the development of two distinct forms of centering prayer.

28. Timothy Ware, ed., *The Art of Prayer: An Orthodox Anthology* (London: Faber and Faber, 1966), 28.

29. Louis Savary and Patricia Berne, *Kything* (New York: Paulist Press, 1988).

30. Theophan the Recluse, quoted in Ware, ed., *The Art of Prayer,* 195.

# CHAPTER THREE

# PRACTICING IMAGINATION

*Ellen Ott Marshall*

For some years now, I have listened to voices of nonviolence. As a student in a peace studies program, I had the good fortune to take a course entitled "Voices of Nonviolence" with John Howard Yoder. We listened to Leo Tolstoy, Mahatma Gandhi, Martin Luther King Jr., Dorothy Day, and the Mothers of the Disappeared. Now I teach a course with the same title. In addition to the voices I listened to as a student, we also listen to the villagers of Le Chambon-sur-Lignon, to Archbishop Oscar Romero, Archbishop Desmond Tutu, Thich Nhat Hanh, and Vaclav Havel. All of them have much to teach us. From their different contexts, they have been involved not only in resistance, but also in construction. They have worked to clear away the debris of cruelty, hatred, and distrust and to foster seeds of compassion, kindness, and hope. Theirs is an act of cultivation, and anyone who has spent two minutes in a garden knows that it is all about the process. You reap what you sow. These voices teach us that intentions matter. Means matter.

Each of these voices heard the challenge that their means were unrealistic and inefficient, not suited to the realities of the world they occupied. And, certainly, our time is filled with other voices of nonviolence whose acts of cultivation are met with the same criticism. When they are feeling generous, the critics acknowledge that these peaceful means are noble, but not realistic given the way things really are. When frustration replaces generosity, the critics accuse the gardeners of being irresponsible. The criticism is understandable because the actions of nonviolent resisters do not fit the situation. But that is precisely the point, is it not? They find themselves in a situation that offers two choices, fight back in kind or acquiesce — but they choose the unexpected third way of nonviolent resistance.[1] So how is it that they see the third way, and what enables them to abide by it when the realities of their context advise otherwise?

I believe that they gain this vision and fortitude by exercising the imagination. One of the many extraordinary characteristics of these voices of nonviolence is that they are able to envision alternatives. This vision gives them a revolutionary sensibility, charged with the belief that the way things are is not the way they must be. In addition to alternate ends, such people are able to envision alternate means. Studies of nonviolent resistance reveal tremendous creativity. Alternatives to violence and to acquiescence abound in the imaginations of these individuals. But the imagination seems to perform another function as well. It serves to remind these people of their connections to the other. In other words, they not only envision the third way between the two givens of violence and acquiescence, but also perceive the connection between the two sides of "us and them."

This chapter focuses on imaginative practices of two voices of nonviolence. Elise Boulding was born in Norway in 1920 and remains an active, leading figure in the field of peace and conflict studies, having published her most recent book, *Cultures of Peace,* in 2000. She served on the faculty of the University of Colorado and later chaired the sociology department at Dartmouth. She also chaired the Women's International League for Peace and Freedom and cofounded the International Peace Research Association with her husband, Kenneth, who passed away in 1993. Elise Boulding was greatly influenced by a Dutch historian named Fred Polak, who "documented how societies' images of the future have empowered their action in the present." While translating his text *Images of the Future* into English, Boulding became convinced that "people can't work for what they can't imagine."[2] In that spirit, she developed a workshop in 1980 entitled "Imaging a World without Weapons." Today, this workshop is adapted and used in a variety of settings, from elementary schools to retreats to conferences.[3] The workshop invites participants to envision a future world of peace in as much detail as possible, to share it with others, to identify one step toward it, and to pledge to take that one step. To my mind, this is an exercise of the prophetic imagination, the power we all have to envision a new world that critiques the present and buoys the spirit for change. This is a practice of peacebuilding with hope.

Thich Nhat Hanh, the second voice in this chapter, is a Buddhist monk who was exiled from his home country of Vietnam because he would not side with either the communist or anticommunist forces.[4] He is most known for his teachings on engaged Buddhism, meditative practices that prepare one to engage the world with loving-kindness. I will focus on his nonduality meditations, which enable one to perceive connections between self and other and to even glimpse the world from the other's point of view. Nonduality meditation is an exercise of the moral imagination, the power that we all have to bind our lives with others and remember the partiality of our own perspectives. This is a practice of peacebuilding with humility.

## THE PROPHETIC IMAGINATION

The imagination is that faculty which enables us to picture people, places, and occurrences that are not immediately present or accessible to us through the senses. I sit in a conference room, listen to mundane discussions, smell stale coffee, and see cream-colored walls and nondescript office furniture. But I am imagining a walk on the beach, the sound of the waves, the smell of the salty sea, and the shimmer of the sun on the water. The imagination enables me to transcend immediate surroundings and place myself elsewhere. Fortunately, this limber faculty can be put to more noble pursuits than my effort to escape a boring meeting in a stale environment. This essay reflects on two visionaries who refuse to let the conditions of the world they experience dictate the parameters of a world they imagine.

However, the imagination can also devise plots that issue in cruelty. We could look to history's despots to know this, but an honest self-assessment reveals it as well. How often have we felt betrayed or witnessed the pain of a loved one and imagined vengeance on the wrongdoer? Another kind of vision comes to those of us who are prone to worry. How often have we waited for a phone to ring and imagined a terrible accident on the freeway? It cannot be claimed, therefore, that the imagination always issues in happy thoughts, social improvements, and peaceful visions. The imagination is just as capable of envisioning pain, dehumanizing the other, and plotting destruction.[5] Indeed, we cannot speak of the connection between the imagination and peace-building without acknowledging the contributions that the imagination has made to war-making as well. The imagination yields weapons of mass destruction, fuels propaganda campaigns, and exacerbates fear.

However, the purpose of this essay is not to examine the hostile imagination, but to highlight two imaginative practices that can contribute to a more peaceable world. Each practice exercises a slightly different aspect of the imagination, one prophetic and the other moral. This distinction between the prophetic and the moral imagination is not a formal one, and I certainly do not mean to suggest that the prophetic imagination lacks morality and the moral imagination lacks a prophetic quality. But I do find these different qualifiers helpful because they emphasize distinct aspects of the imagination. The prophetic imagination emphasizes the sight beyond experience. The moral imagination emphasizes the perception of connections beneath fragmentation.

Before delving into this distinction, let me offer one general comment about the connection between the imagination and ethics, which is my particular field of study. One of the foundational claims of ethics is that agency (the power to act) requires a goal, or an end, as Aristotle would say. For example, I just took a break to get a cup of coffee. Post-lunch drowsiness threatened to set in, and I really need to finish this portion of the chapter. I know that caffeine can help me wake up again. So, I act (I leave my office and go to the community center downstairs for coffee) in order to wake up and work more productively. Agency requires a goal. Everything tends toward an end.

But that was an easy example. The goal itself was clear, to wake up, and the means, coffee, is a quantity known all too well. What if I find myself with a need, but I don't know how to fill it? Or what if I have a need, but its redress is out of my reach? When that which is needed is either out of reach or out of sight, my power to act is diminished. Agency requires a sense of the possible. The link to the imagination surfaces at this point, for it enlarges our sense of the possible. In the poetic language of William Lynch, imagination is "the gift that constantly proposes to itself that the boundaries of the possible are wider than they seem."[6]

Without the imagination, we become trapped in the "prison of the instant," Lynch suggests. That is, a portion of our experience becomes absolutized such that we are no longer able to see it as one moment among many. The imagination liberates us from such moments, not by denying their existence, but by placing them in relative proportion to others. This moment is one among many, and the many hold potential that the one does not. Thus, "the imagination will always be the enemy of the absolutizing instinct and the ally of hope," concludes Lynch.[7]

We see why an individual's imagination so threatens those who wish to maintain the status quo. It constantly proposes that the boundaries of the possible are not what they seem. It "refuses the present impasse."[8] It fuels the revolutionary sentiment by suggesting that the way things are is not the way they must be. Prophetically speaking, the imagination envisions alternatives, which both critique the present and inspire

agency. Prophets, whether they communicate to us through texts or
rise up from today's marginalized communities, challenge those pieces
of reality that have been absolutized. These are the voices that inspire
us because they alert us to the potential for change. In Walter Brueggemann's words, they remind us of "promises yet to be kept, promises that
stand in judgment of the present."[9] Invariably, prophets describe a vision that is unreasonable, even absurd. Thus, Brueggemann contends,
"*prophetic* must be *imaginative* because it is urgently out beyond the
ordinary."[10]

The unreasonableness of the prophetic imagination is a central
theme in a more recent text by Mary Grey, appropriately titled *The
Outrageous Pursuit of Hope*. Like Brueggemann, Grey insists that the
prophetic imagination is a "public imagination, belonging to the public domain, inspiring the full range of communities belonging to it
to commitment to fuller visions of well-being."[11] The outrageous nature of the prophetic imagination is not confined to its vision alone,
but rather extends to a community's commitment to live it out. In
Grey's words, "prophetic imagination *is outrageous* — not merely in
dreaming the dream, but in already living out of the dream before
it has come to pass, and in embodying this dream in concrete actions."[12] We find, therefore, the suggestion that the prophet not only
inspires the community, but rises from it. As Brueggemann notes, the
scriptures suggest that "God can 'raise up prophets'... in any circumstance." However, one can mark characteristics of a subcommunity
that seems to provide the prophet's "natural habitat." One such char-
acteristic is "an active practice of hope," kept alive by the awareness
of promises not yet fulfilled.[13] It is crucial to take note of this social component. We may hesitate to claim that a community in which
we participate might give rise to a prophet, but we can embrace and
act upon the conviction that our community might give rise to the
prophetic imagination.

Through the writings of Lynch, Brueggemann, and Grey, we find a
nice web emerging. We now see the prophetic imagination as entwined

with agency, for it frees us from the prison of the instant so that we might regain the power to act. We find that the prophetic imagination is intimately related to hope because it enables us to envision alternatives and recover a sense of the possible. And we find that the prophetic imagination has a vital social component not only because it inspires others, but also because it emerges from collective commitments to enact a dream. Unfortunately, our North American society does not seem to encourage the prophetic imagination. We value realistic steps in a process much more highly than outrageous visions. And yet, our broken and violent world is in dire need of outrageous visions, unreasonable hopes, and unwavering commitments to unrealistic dreams. Elise Boulding's imaging workshop offers one way to exercise the prophetic imagination, one way to practice living in this web of imagination, agency, hope, and community.

## ELISE BOULDING: ENVISIONING EXERCISES

I had the good fortune to take part in one of Elise Boulding's imaging workshops during a peace studies symposium at Tufts University in the spring of 2000. I had never participated in something like this before. And I was not sure that I would feel comfortable even closing my eyes in public, let alone imagining a world that I would then describe to others. Across my mind flashed every criticism I have ever heard (and some I have expressed) about idealistic peace activists who have lost touch with reality. However, I have great respect for Elise Boulding and was somewhat stunned to be in the same room with her. So, when this wise and unwavering woman told me to close my eyes, I did.

Elise Boulding's imaging exercise is a social practice. I do think that one could engage certain steps alone and find them meaningful, but there is particular power in the social dimension of this practice. In one step, we not only share our image with others, but also become aware of a variety of peaceful visions. That sharing step reveals common longings and creative proposals. It leaves the participants with a feeling of solidarity and encouragement. In the final step, each participant contributes one idea to a large basket. This offering embodies Margaret Mead's oft-quoted reminder: "Never doubt that a small group of thoughtful, committed citizens can change the world. Indeed, it is the only thing that ever has."

The practice proceeds through three general stages. First, we imagine a world that is truly peaceful. Then we describe that world to others. And, finally, we identify one thing (no matter how small) that we could do today to help us move closer to that vision.

*Imagine a World:* Picture yourself approaching a hedge. You hear sounds on the other side of the hedge and part the branches to peek through. The peaceful world you imagine is there. What does it look like? Who is there? If you see people, what do they look like? What are they doing? Let your mind explore every detail of the scene. If people are talking, can you hear what they are saying? What do the natural surroundings look like? Are there buildings or other human-made structures? What do they look like? Is it a particular time of day? A particular season? When you are satisfied that you have imagined this world in as much detail as possible — when you can see, hear, and feel every piece of it clearly — open your eyes.

*Describe the World:* Create images to help others visualize the world you imagine. Even if you consider yourself a terrible artist, as I do, it is helpful to record your vision pictorially. The pictures you create may not do the image justice, but drawing will help to clarify the image in your head and to bring remaining details into focus. The images you record, no matter how metaphorical or abstract, will also help you communicate your vision to others.

When you have depicted as much of your world as you can, gather with a few other people. Take time with each picture. Explain yours as carefully as possible. You will be tempted to apologize for either your artistic ability or the unrealistic vision that you are sharing. Do not apologize. As you listen to your peers describe their vision, ask whatever questions you need to ask in order to see that vision as clearly as they do. You may be tempted to take issue with elements of their vision. Do not criticize.

*Identify a Step:* Return now to your own seat and once again close your eyes. Return to the hedge, part the branches, and picture your world again. This time, focus on the differences between the world you envision and the world you live in. Choose one difference to reflect on in more detail. For example, let your mind's eye rest on one image that symbolizes a great improvement over the world you live in. What would need to happen in this world in order to realize that piece of your vision? Brainstorm freely. Try not to censor your own suggestions, but let them flow uninhibited. Now, filter through that list for one thing that you could do. It does not matter how small it is as long as it is one thing that you could do to move this world toward your vision. Write down the one thing that you will do.

In the closing step of this practice, the facilitator presents a basket and invites participants to contribute their one thing to it. In my memory of the workshop at Tufts, I see Elise Boulding standing in the front of the auditorium with a big basket full of little slips of paper. And I imagine that those slips of paper said things like, "Be nicer to people who bug me" and "Bike to work" and "Turn off the water while I brush my teeth" and "Take twelve students to a developing country every spring semester" and "Spend one hour a week tutoring a woman who needs to get her GED" and "Vote." The sum of this experience was a movement from imagination to critique to agency. We envisioned a world that we cannot see. We talked about the difference between that world and the one we know. And we named *and pledged to do* one thing that would close the gap a bit. We exercised the prophetic imagination and were rewarded with a buoyed spirit and a feeling of empowerment.

## THE MORAL IMAGINATION

As we move now to a discussion of the moral imagination, I want to stress that this is not a formal distinction. There is no universally agreed-upon, formal classification of the imagination into these two categories. The "moral imagination" is most often used to describe the role of the imagination in the moral life generally. According to this usage, the prophetic imagination might be placed under the umbrella of the moral imagination, for it serves to generate agency and sustain hope, two features essential to the moral life. However, I use these two different qualifiers, prophetic and moral, to designate slightly different functions. As we have seen, the prophetic imagination enables us to transcend the particularities of our current situation in order to envision alternatives, alternatives that serve to critique the present and generate action for change. The moral imagination also allows us to transcend the particularities of our individual situation, for this is the basic function of the imagination, giving us a picture of things not currently accessible through the senses. But the purpose of the moral imagination is a bit different, to my mind. Where the prophetic imagination offers us radically new visions, the moral imagination gives different perspectives on the familiar. Through the moral imagination, we see our world in a new way. The elements within our scope of vision remain the same, but we rearrange them such that our perspective is fundamentally altered.

To help with this description, I turn to *Christian Ethics and Imagination* by Philip S. Keane. Keane uses the moral imagination more broadly than I do, but his description of its nature and function resonates with my understanding of the effect of Thich Nhat Hanh's meditative practices. Keane begins by referencing two forms of knowledge.[14] With the first, sense knowledge, we learn through concrete, particular experience. I learned how to grow a seed in a cup in grade school. I learned that the seed needed plenty of good soil, water, and sunlight. Although my thumb is not as green as others', I do know the basics of plant care. And I learned them (and continue to learn them) through concrete interaction with seeds, soil, water, and sunlight. But I also take those concrete lessons and extrapolate metaphors. Indeed, I used one such metaphor to open this chapter: "Anyone who has spent two minutes in a garden knows that it is all about the process. You reap what you sow." In drawing this lesson, I have put into practice a second kind of knowledge, one that is more abstract and tends toward universal claims. We learn by employing both forms of knowledge: sense knowledge and abstract knowledge.

Philip Keane suggests that imagination enables us to weave these two forms of knowledge together. In his words, "imagination can be described as the basic process by which we draw together the concrete and the universal elements of our human experience."[15] From my concrete garden experience, I infer that means matter. And I go so far as to suggest that in every situation the process on which we embark affects its outcome. I have moved from a concrete experience to a universal claim. Teachers tend to move in the opposite direction regularly. That is, we begin with an abstract concept that we want to share with others, and we turn to concrete experiences that help us to explain the abstract idea. This is exactly what I just did. I wanted to tell you about the two forms of knowledge. And so I turned to my grade school experience (and probably yours too) as an example of sense knowledge. Both moves, from concrete to universal and from theoretical to sensual, involve the imagination.

Drawing on the work of Paul Ricoeur, Keane describes this process as playful. We allow the two forms of knowledge to play off of one another and open ourselves to the insights that emerge. Indeed, we suspend judgment during this process, avoiding preconceived notions that might simply reinforce previous learning rather than open us to new perspectives. Keane insists that this process leads us to better understanding. "By allowing this interplay between the two aspects of our knowing, we get a much deeper chance to look at what we know, to form a vision of it." Thus, he refines his definition of the moral imagination: "a playful suspension of judgment leading us toward a more appropriate grasp of reality."[16] Through this process, we become increasingly aware of the limits of our own perspective and perhaps the arrogance with which we have projected our perspective onto others.

This is why I associate the moral imagination with humility. By introducing this quality into the discussion, I do not mean to recommend a subservient posture whereby one quietly accepts the world as it is. Nor do I mean to repeat the gross mistake of those who extend the virtue of humility over the heads of oppressed persons in order to maintain control. I recommend humility (and value the moral imagination for fostering it) because violence relies on arrogant certitude. We become so convinced of the surety of our own perspective that we are willing to commit an irreparable act in order to advance it. The moral imagination prompts us to see things differently. Perhaps we think about the unfolding event with a longer-term view, which calls into question the short-term solution. Perhaps we think about the present conflict from the other's perspective, which calls into question our own version of events. The moral imagination — this interplay between concrete and universal — reminds us that our view of this world is partial and influenced by personal prejudice and public propaganda.

I believe that there is an inverse relationship between arrogance and empathy. That is, as I become aware of the partiality of my own perspective, I become more open to the experience of another. By enabling this process, the moral imagination contributes to the task of peacebuilding. Humility and empathy unravel the mechanisms of war. However, in times of heightened conflict, humility and empathy do not come easily. Indeed, our feelings of vulnerability incline us to cling to our own point of view and rally around the national mission. So, we need practices to exercise the moral imagination so that we might cultivate the habit of empathy.

## THICH NHAT HANH: NONDUALITY MEDITATION

As a Buddhist, one of Thich Nhat Hanh's principal concerns is dualism, our tendency to divide the world between us and them, good and bad, right and wrong, friend and enemy. Consequently, many of his meditation exercises aim for nonduality, meaning an understanding of the other and an awareness of the relationship rather than the distance between us. Thich Nhat Hanh describes this awareness of relationship as interbeing. Through Buddhist meditation, one sees that "there is no such thing as an individual."[17] He illustrates this teaching by directing our attention to the "cloud floating in this sheet of paper. Without a cloud there will be no water; without water, the trees cannot grow; and without trees, you cannot make paper."[18] The paper is made up of nonpaper elements. "In the same way, the individual is made up of non-individual elements."[19] Later in this beautiful little book, *Being Peace,* Thich Nhat Hanh returns to this image. "In one sheet of paper, we see everything else, the cloud, the forest, the logger. I am, therefore you are. You are, therefore I am. That is the meaning of the word 'interbeing.' We inter-are."[20]

Practices that make us aware of nonduality help us to address conflict in our personal lives and to take an essential step toward reconciliation between peoples and nations more generally. In this passage written during the cold war, Thich Nhat Hanh explains:

> The situation of the world is still like this. People completely identify with one side, one ideology. To understand the suffering and the fear of a citizen of the Soviet Union, we have to become one with him or her. To do so is dangerous — we will be suspected by both sides. But if we don't do it, if we align ourselves with one side or the other, we will lose our chance to work for peace. Reconciliation is to understand both sides, to go to one side and describe the suffering being endured by the other side, and then to go to the other side and describe the suffering being endured by the first side.[21]

In order to overcome duality, Thich Nhat Hanh calls us to practice imagining ourselves as the other. This does not mean that I will agree with everything the other person has done. But it does mean that I will see the humanity in that person and the connection between us. Remember, there is no such thing as an individual. My identity, my being, is thoroughly wrapped up with yours. We "inter-are." Meditation makes us mindful of these connections.

One of the most meaningful items to come to me via email after the attack on the World Trade Center on September 11, 2001, was a poem attributed to Thich Nhat Hanh entitled "Rest in Peace." I have since learned that this poem was written by Frederic and Mary Ann Brussat, who were inspired by Thich Nhat Hanh's poem "Please Call Me by My True Names." Both of these poems are beautiful illustrations of non-duality and can serve as the basis for practicing the moral imagination. I have chosen to use the Brussats' poem here because their images are particularly challenging to me. As with imaging workshops, this practice can be done alone or with a group. I have, most frequently, used the poem with groups to demonstrate nonduality. However, I also benefit from meditating on it alone to practice nonduality.

*Preparation:* First, it is helpful to recall the purpose of this practice. According to Thich Nhat Hanh's teaching, one does not meditate in order to withdraw from the world, but rather to prepare to engage it more fully. Indeed, such withdrawal is impossible because you, the individual, are made up of nonindividual elements. We always carry the world with us. Meditation does not draw us out of the world, but prepares us to live in the world. Thus, the first step of preparation is to remember: "When you meditate, it is not just for yourself, you do it for the whole society."[22] This particular practice benefits society by alerting us to our own misperceptions, sensitizing us to the views of others, and fostering understanding and empathy.

If you are practicing alone, take some time to prepare yourself for meditation. Find a quiet place and adopt a comfortable sitting position. Close your eyes and relax. If you are leading or participating in a group, recognize that people have various levels of comfort with public practices of spirituality. Some may be most comfortable listening with their eyes open, while others prefer a prayerful posture. Be sure that the purpose and context of the poem are clear to everyone.

*The text:* Below is a copy of the poem in its entirety. You may choose to meditate on one stanza at a time, committing it to memory and repeating it several times, or you may choose to read through the entire poem at once, reflecting on the variety of images. There may also be some stanzas that challenge you more than others, and you may choose to work with them repeatedly. If you are working with a group, you may choose to read the poem aloud to them or to take turns so that the group participates in the reading and hears each stanza in a different voice. Again, recognize that some people may prefer not to read, and be sure to give them the option to pass.

## "REST IN PEACE"

*I am a World Trade Center tower, standing tall in the clear blue sky, feeling a violent blow in my side, and I am a towering inferno of pain and suffering imploding upon myself and collapsing to the ground. May I rest in peace.*

*I am a terrified passenger on a hijacked airplane not knowing where we are going or that I am riding on fuel tanks that will be instruments of death, and I am a worker arriving at my office not knowing that in just a moment my future will be obliterated. May I rest in peace.*

*I am a pigeon on the plaza between the two towers eating crumbs from someone's breakfast when fire rains down on me from the skies, and I am a bed of flowers admired daily by thousands of tourists now buried under five stories of rubble. May I rest in peace.*

*I am a firefighter sent into dark corridors of smoke and debris on a mission of mercy only to have it collapse around me, and I am a rescue worker risking my life to save lives who is very aware that I may not make it out alive. May I rest in peace.*

*I am a survivor who has fled down the stairs and out of the building to safety who knows that nothing will ever be the same in my soul again, and I am a doctor in a hospital treating patients burned from head to toe who* knows that these horrible images will remain in my mind forever. May I know peace.

I am a tourist in Times Square looking up at the giant TV screens thinking I'm seeing a disaster movie as I watch the Twin Towers crash to the ground, and I am a New York woman sending e-mails to friends and family letting them know that I am safe. May I know peace.

I am a piece of paper that was on someone's desk this morning and now I am debris scattered by the wind across lower Manhattan, and I am a stone in the graveyard at Trinity Church covered with soot from the buildings that once stood proudly above me, death meeting death. May I rest in peace.

I am a dog sniffing in the rubble for signs of life, doing my best to be of service, and I am a blood donor waiting in line to make a simple but very needed contribution for the victims. May I know peace.

I am a resident in an apartment in downtown New York who has been forced to evacuate my home, and I am a resident in an apartment uptown who has walked a hundred blocks home in a stream of other refugees. May I know peace.

I am a family member who has just learned that someone I love has died, and I am a pastor who must comfort someone who has suffered a heart-breaking loss. May I know peace.

I am a loyal American who feels violated and vows to stand behind any military action it takes to wipe terrorists off the face of the earth, and I am a loyal American who feels violated and worries that people who look and sound like me are all going to be blamed for this tragedy. May I know peace.

I am a frightened city dweller who wonders whether I'll ever feel safe in a skyscraper again, and I am a pilot who wonders whether there will ever be a way to make the skies truly safe. May I know peace.

I am the owner of a small store with five employees that has been put out of business by this tragedy, and I am an executive in a multinational corporation who is concerned about the cost of doing business in a terrorized world. May I know peace.

I am a visitor to New York City who purchases postcards of the World Trade Center Twin Towers that are no more, and I am a television reporter trying to put into words the terrible things I have seen. May I know peace.

I am a boy in New Jersey waiting for a father who will never come home, and I am a boy in a faraway country rejoicing in the streets of my village because someone has hurt the hated Americans. May I know peace.

I am a general talking into the microphones about how we must stop the terrorist cowards who have perpetrated this heinous crime, and I am an intelligence officer trying to discern how such a thing could have happened on American soil, and I am a city official trying to find ways to alleviate the suffering of my people. May I know peace.

I am a terrorist whose hatred for America knows no limit and I am willing to die to prove it, and I am a terrorist sympathizer standing with all the enemies of American capitalism and imperialism, and I am a master strategist for a terrorist group who planned this abomination. My heart is not yet capable of openness, tolerance, and loving. May I know peace.

I am a citizen of the world glued to my television set, fighting back my rage and despair at these horrible events, and I am a person of faith struggling to forgive the unforgivable, praying for the consolation of those who have lost loved ones, calling upon the merciful beneficence of God/Lord/Allah/Spirit/ Higher Power. May I know peace.

*Reflection:* Give yourself and your group time to reflect on the experience of reading, hearing, or saying these words, especially the first time you work with them. Were there some stanzas that were markedly more difficult for you? What makes them so difficult? What images or personal experiences does the reading trigger for you? Are there stanzas that you would add, given developments in the world or your personal life since September 2001? If you continue to work with the poem over time, you might reflect on how your reading changes. Do you focus on different stanzas, individuals, or details with each reading? Are there passages that gain meaning the more you read them? Do the difficult ones get easier? And perhaps most important, given the purpose of the practice, how does the poem affect the way you see your world? Does it make a difference in your interactions with others? Does it influence the way you receive the daily news? Does it prompt you to change your behavior in some way?

Earlier, I suggested that one effect of this practice is that it humbles. Now that we have the practice before us, some further comments on humility might be helpful. Such meditation exercises teach us to live in awareness, a fundamental Buddhist principle.[23] As I reflect on the "Rest in Peace" practice, I become more aware of the perception of others and of the deep interrelatedness of all things. Although I immediately sympathize with the boy in New Jersey whose father will never come home, I am becoming aware that the boy in the faraway land has cause to hate us. I too would like to believe the political rhetoric that says, "They hate us because they hate freedom." Such reasoning restores my confidence in my nation as a good and moral place. But like many people, I have tried to examine our country more critically and to listen to others' perceptions of us as arrogant, imperialist, and hypocritical. This is a humbling lesson. But, again, it is not just the content of the lesson that humbles, but the growing awareness of the limitations of my own perspective and my tendency toward misperception.

I have also learned from the "loyal American" who stands "behind any military action it takes to wipe terrorists off the face of the earth." I believe that there is that of God in every person and that war is an act of violence against God's creation. And I believe that terrorism cannot be overcome with war because violence cannot overcome hatred. So, I do not believe that a war against terrorism is either moral or realistic. However, I lived in New York City, and my husband has one of the many near-miss stories of that day. When I recall his shaking voice on our answering machine telling me that he is okay and a coworker screaming in the background as the second plane hit the tower, I am filled with fear and rage. And I know that I am related to the "loyal American" seeking vengeance and reassurance through violence. This awareness of interrelatedness humbles me. I must recognize my own capacity for hatred and for harm. This exercise reminds me that I am the other and the other is me. In order to see that, I need to suspend my preconceived notions and enable the interplay between my sense experience and universal claims. This is an exercise of the moral imagination, and it fosters humility.

## CONCLUSION

We have now before us two aspects of the imagination, each with a corresponding exercise and effect. While I intended this categorization to be helpful for explanatory purposes, I do realize that the imaginative, emotive, and peacebuilding processes will most likely be much more fluid than this. For example, while one reader's spirit may be buoyed by her prophetic imagination, she may also feel humbled by the task that stretches ahead of her. While another reader may feel humbled when his awareness of the other's perception increases, he may also feel encouraged by the potential for empathy and understanding that arises. My main purpose for discussing these characteristics is not to dictate the affective result of the imaginative practice, but to suggest that peacebuilding requires hope and humility, both of which can be fostered by the imagination.

Peacebuilding requires a truthful assessment of the way things are, not as individual perception or national propaganda depicts them, but as the rich tapestry of human experience presents them. We need to acknowledge the capacity for good and the capacity for harm that rests in all of us rather than divide the globe into those who love freedom and those who form the axis of evil. We need to recognize that perceptions vary and even contradict one another, and that the truth most likely rests somewhere between them. And we must admit that life is fragile, even when that awareness of vulnerability clashes with our national image. The moral imagination pushes us toward these lessons by suspending our preconceived notions, personal preferences, and national allegiances so that we might consider another point of view or the deep connection underneath fragmentation or the self and state beneath appearances.

Peacebuilding also requires a vision of the way things could be. As Professor Boulding suggests, we cannot work for what we cannot imagine. The prophetic imagination gives us, among other things, the power to act. I am afraid that we have a tendency to wait for the next prophetic voice to offer us a vision and enliven the movement for peace. Marian Wright Edelman made this point beautifully in a speech a few years ago. She thanks her audience for being there because "so many people are waiting for Gandhi to come back, or Dr. King to come back. They're not. We're it!"[24] She is right. It is up to us to remake this world. We must be accountable to the realities of our current situation, and we must also be accountable to visions of a time when no one will hurt or destroy in all God's holy mountain. We must be accountable to a world where history repeats itself and to a God who is even now doing a new thing. If we are to build on the work of voices of nonviolence, we must embrace hope, walk humbly, and practice imagination.

## NOTES

1. This language of the "third way" is used by many nonviolent resisters. For those interested in the connection between this language and the Christian tradition, see Walter Wink, "Jesus' Third Way," in *Transforming Violence: Linking Local and Global Peacemaking*, ed. Robert Herr and Judy Zimmerman Herr (Scottdale, Pa.: Herald Press, 1998), 34–47.

2. Elise Boulding, *Cultures of Peace: The Hidden Side of History* (Syracuse: Syracuse University Press, 2000), 29.

3. Boulding's 1990 text, *Building a Global Civic Culture*, contains a description of the workshop process as an appendix: "A Workbook for Imagining a World without Weapons" (Syracuse: Syracuse University Press, 1990), 172–76.

She also commented on the need for broadening the workshop to include non-Western influences in 1991. See Elise Boulding, "The Challenge of Imaging Peace in Wartime," *Conflict Resolution Notes* 8 (April 1991): 34–36.

4. As this book goes to press, Thich Nhat Hanh is visiting Vietnam. From January 12 to April 11, 2005, he is traveling with a hundred monastics and ninety lay friends and teaching in four different areas of the country. For information about this trip, go to the Web site for Plum Village Meditation Center: www.plumvillage.org/tnhvntrip/AboutTNHVNTrip.htm.

5. Sam Keen's text *Faces of the Enemy: Reflections of the Hostile Imagination* testifies to the "hostile imagination" (San Francisco: Harper & Row, 1986).

6. William F. Lynch, *Images of Hope: Imagination as Healer of the Hopeless* (Notre Dame, Ind.: University of Notre Dame Press, 1965), 35.

7. Ibid., 36, 243.

8. Mary C. Grey, *The Outrageous Pursuit of Hope: Prophetic Dreams for the Twenty-First Century* (New York: Crossroad, 2000), 43.

9. Walter Brueggemann, *The Prophetic Imagination,* 2nd ed. (Minneapolis: Fortress Press, 2001), xvi.

10. Ibid., xv.

11. Grey, *The Outrageous Pursuit of Hope*, 43.

12. Ibid.

13. Brueggemann, *The Prophetic Imagination,* xvi.

14. Philip S. Keane, *Christian Ethics and Imagination* (New York: Paulist Press, 1984), 79–80.

15. Ibid., 81.

16. Ibid.

17. Thich Nhat Hanh, *Being Peace* (Berkeley: Parallax Press, 1987, 1996), 45.

18. Ibid., 45–46.

19. Ibid., 47.

20. Ibid., 87.

21. Ibid., 70.

22. Ibid., 47.

23. Ibid., 65.

24. Marian Wright Edelman, "Caring Enough to Build a World of Peace," *Fellowship* (January–February 2001): 4–5.

# CHAPTER FOUR

# LOVING OUR ENEMIES

### Contributions of the Narrative Arts to a Practice of Peacebuilding

*Frank Rogers Jr.*

What is an Al Qaeda terrorist doing in heaven? How do you love a drunk driver who has killed your only child? How is the person who most pushes our buttons our greatest spiritual ally? The imaginative freedom of the narrative arts allows us to engage such questions with promising, sometimes surprising, results. Storytelling, playmaking, stage drama, and creative writing are venues through which the moral imagination can be stimulated, creative action can be envisioned, insights about the life of faith can be generated, and peacemaking skills can be practiced. In particular, these art forms help us wrestle with one of the most challenging, and most vital, practices of Christian peacebuilding. How do we respond to violence with nonviolent compassion? In short, how do we love our enemies?

## SETTING THE STAGE: JESUS' NONVIOLENT INVITATION

Walter Wink declares that loving our enemies is the most pressing political imperative facing the survival of our planet. It is also the central spiritual invitation offered to people of faith. "There is, in fact, no other way to God for our time but through the enemy, for loving the enemy has become the key both to human survival in the nuclear age and to personal transformation."[1] This social mandate and spiritual opportunity is counterintuitive. Our enemies are those who mean us harm. And when we are attacked, verbally, emotionally, physically, our instinct is to retaliate. Such retaliation goads greater enmity, prompting further retaliation. A Russian folktale illustrates this familiar cycle of violence.

> Two merchants have become bitter enemies. They spread malicious rumors about one another, they steal each other's customers, they sabotage one another's shops until, driven by their reciprocating rage, they square off in the middle of town. One shopkeeper bares his fists at the other. The second draws a knife. The first counters with a samurai's sword. The second pulls out a pistol. The first comes back with a rifle. The second whisks out a dynamite stick. The first barrels forth with a dynamite bundle and defiantly lights the fuse. Finally an angel, grieving the depth of vengeance and alarmed at the escalating violence, intervenes. She snuffs out the fuse of the first man, then parlays with him on the side. She tells him that she is prepared to grant him any wish in the world — extravagant riches, abundant children, a king's palace, anything he desires at all...with one condition. Whatever he wishes for himself, she will also grant to his rival, twofold. The shopkeeper muses over the dilemma, desiring wealth yet bitter at the prospect of his rival's double share. Finally, he knows what he wants. He turns to the angel and confirms, "Whatever I wish for, my rival will receive twofold?" The angel nods. "Then what I want for myself is, one blind eye."[2]

Originally, the Hebrew law "An eye for an eye and a tooth for a tooth" was designed to curb escalating violence. Instead of massacring an entire tribe when a band of marauders attacks a village, the village's just retaliation was limited to a life for a life, an eye for an eye. But such a limit, as seen in the folktale, is difficult to maintain. If someone hits me, I want to hit them back...*harder.* If a terrorist attacks me, I want to obliterate them, *and their friends.* Violence breeds heightened violence. And at the end of the day, as Tevye from *Fiddler on the Roof* foresaw, the world ends up blind and toothless.

Jesus, in the Sermon on the Mount, taught a new way. "You have heard that it was said, 'An eye for an eye and a tooth for a tooth.' But I say to you, Do not resist an evildoer. But if anyone strikes you on the right cheek, turn the other also.... You have heard that it was said, 'You shall love your neighbor and hate your enemy.' But I say to you, Love your enemies and pray for those that persecute you" (Matt. 5:38–39, 43–44). Such words seem demanding to the point of absurdity. Is it really possible to simply turn the other cheek when met with violence? What does it mean to love our enemies? Role-playing this text yields insight.[3]

Often Jesus' teaching is understood as a form of naive passivity — if someone strikes you once, roll over and let them strike you again. Such a response *is* naive. Telling a battered woman to submit to further assault from her husband is a violation of the woman's safety and her dignity. It is also a violation of Jesus' teaching.

Susan and Cathy, two high school youth in a dramatic arts program, volunteered to role-play the passage enjoining Christians to "turn the other cheek." They squared off onstage where I asked Susan (*in slow motion!*) to hit Cathy in the face. Susan reached back in a mock impersonation of a heavyweight prizefighter and commenced to slug Cathy. I stopped her midway. "What is wrong with this reenactment?" I asked the other teens. They observed that the text cites being struck on the *right* cheek. Susan was striking Cathy's *left* cheek, as any right-handed punch or open-handed slap would do. So Susan fisted her left hand and prepared to belt Cathy on the right cheek. I stopped them again. I explained that in first-century society, the left hand was reserved for unclean tasks. To even wave it carried a stiff penalty, let alone touching another person with it. Susan tried again. The only way she could strike Cathy's right cheek was with a backhanded slap. The teens recognized that such a slap was less an act of aggression and more an act of humiliation. Susan was insulting Cathy. In a society where honor was paramount, to strike an equal in such a degrading way carried an exorbitant fine. The situation Jesus assumed clearly involved a person in a position of power striking an inferior with the intent of humiliating them — a master to a slave, a Roman to a Jew, etc.

Instinctively, the victim Cathy had two options, fight or flight. She considered the more satisfying option of hitting Susan back, but if she retaliated, returned violence with violence, she would suffer severe retribution. She considered swallowing it and walking away, but then she would surrender herself to the indignity. So she tried Jesus' third way. She "turned the other cheek." Literally. She took her face from being slapped sideways and turned her head such that her left cheek was thrust prominently in Susan's face. Immediately, everything about Cathy changed. She stood up straighter. She was centered and solid. A boldness beamed from her face displaying an empowered dignity. Nonverbally, she was saying, "Try again — your first blow tried to humiliate me but I refuse to let you." Susan, the aggressor, was suddenly placed on the defensive. She couldn't strike Cathy with another backhanded slap, as Cathy's right cheek was hidden behind the bold position of her left cheek in Susan's face. She couldn't strike Cathy with her fist as such would acknowledge Cathy as a peer, a victory in itself for the victim. Susan intended to humiliate Cathy, but Cathy had effectively stripped Susan of the power to dehumanize her. In doing so, she practiced Gandhi's teaching, "The first principle of nonviolent action is that of noncooperation with everything humiliating."[4] Discovering her dignity, she inspires others to stand up for their own as well.

James Lawson, a nonviolent activist with Martin Luther King, recounts an example of such a disarming response during the civil rights movement. Rev. Lawson was leaving a café in the rural South when a passing motorcyclist spat into his face, then pulled into a parking lot across the street. Rev. Lawson wiped the spit off with his handkerchief, walked over to the cyclist, and with dignified nonchalance, asked the cyclist for directions to a nearby town. The nonplussed motorcyclist knew of nothing else to do but give the guy directions as if Lawson were his social equal.

Turning the other cheek to one who acts violently is hardly an exercise in masochistic passivity. Jesus' nonviolent invitation is an empowered form of action that refuses to be humiliated, claims one's dignity in the face of dehumanization, seizes the initiative, and invites the aggressor into an appropriate mutual relationship. Such action may be dangerous: a master may beat the insolence out of a slave turning the other cheek, a motorcyclist may blow up in rage. But the action is not a cowering acquiescence to an oppressive situation. Turning the other cheek is standing up for dignity.

As if such courageous action was not challenging enough, Jesus offers an additional twist. We are invited to nonviolently resist the one who does us evil *and* . . . love them while we are doing it. As Wink observes, "Without love for enemies, nonviolence would be just another arrow in the quiver of coercive force."[5] Reverend Lawson's mentor responded to this invitation as well.

In 1963, Martin Luther King paid a trip to Birmingham, Alabama, reputed to be the most segregated city this side of Johannesburg. One evening, he spoke at a church. The place was packed. People filled the pews and the aisles, the window alcoves and balconies; even the parking lot was fitted with speakers for the overflowing crowd. As King stepped to the podium, a white man in the front row stood up and walked toward him. Not until the man was quite close did King see the hatred in his eyes. The man lunged after King, knocked him back onto the floor, and beat him on the chest. The church erupted. A mob swarmed around King, grabbed the attacker, and herded him toward the door. Cries rang out, "Kill the bastard! Lynch him! Beat him to a bloody pulp!" In the midst of all the chaos, Martin Luther King staggered up and boomed his baritone voice through the microphone.

*"Stop!"*

The place fell silent. King walked over to the man, put his arm around the assailant's shoulder, and looked around the crowd. "What do you want to do with this man? Kill him? Beat him? Do unto him what he's done unto us? That isn't our task. Our task is to step into his shoes. To ask ourselves, 'What would we be like if everybody we knew, our parents and ministers and teachers, taught us since we could walk that the Negro was a thing?' Our task is to see the hatred in his eyes and refuse to mirror it ourselves, to feel his fear and glimpse his goodness, and show him what it means to be a human being welcomed into the beloved community that holds us all."

Martin Luther King may have saved a man's life that day. He certainly challenged us all with the peacebuilding practice of loving our enemies. How might we practice such radical love in today's world? Using the narrative arts, I have asked people of faith to engage this question. I invited them to write stories, create plays, and improvise real-life scenarios around this practice. I asked them to use their creativity. I asked them to wrestle with the real tensions and difficulties that emerge. Above all, I asked them to be honest.

They took me at my word. Below are three narrative pieces that illuminate important features in the radical practice of loving our enemies, each with an introduction and concluding comments.[6]

## "TERRORISTS IN HEAVEN": LOVING THE ENEMY THROUGH TELLING ALTERNATIVE STORIES

The practice of Christian peacebuilding involves a clash with formative narratives in our culture. Narrative is the primary form through which human beings make meaning of their experience.[7] Persons, communities, and cultures are engaged on journeys defined by the various ends asserted by formative narratives. We may quest for true love, the American dream, the kin-dom of God, the blessing of Allah, global democracy, or multinational capitalistic domination, depending on the narratives that shape us. Other people, communities, and cultures are interpreted as allies or enemies to the extent to which they promote or threaten such quests. How we engage those who threaten our pursuits, our "enemies" as it were, is also shaped by narrative. Stories form us toward either violent or nonviolent engagement with such people.

Walter Wink argues that violence, not Christianity, is the true religion of America.[8] This religion is sanctioned by an insidious but pervasive narrative, the myth of redemptive violence. The features of this myth are all too well known. An irredeemable and unambiguous "bad guy" threatens without provocation or cause a group of innocent people. Fortunately, an indestructible and unambiguous "good guy," often a superhero of some sort, rallies to the cause. Using violence, not diplomacy, negotiation, or persuasion, the "good guy" completely annihilates the villain, ridding the world of evil in doing so. When the villain is destroyed, order is restored . . . until the next episode, when an equally unambiguous villain returns. Both television and the theater are saturated with such narratives. Children watch Teenage Mutant Ninja Turtles, Power Rangers, and Popeye. Older audiences take in Rambo, James Bond, and the Terminator.

The myth of redemptive violence often informs U.S. responses to those who threaten national security. Such mythology, for example, was used by government leaders to shape the interpretation of the events of 9-11. Al Qaeda terrorists, unambiguously evil, attacked an innocent community with neither provocation nor cause. The terrorists, those countries that harbored them, and the people who sympathized with them were equally unambiguous in their evil, capriciously threatening freedom and the unequivocally good American way of life. The only appropriate response was to use violence to obliterate the world of their presence, thus restoring order and securing the cause of right. A simple matter of good against evil.

Jesus' invitation to love our enemies suggests an alternative narrative by which to interpret such events: the myth of nonviolent redemption instead of the myth of redemptive violence. In the months after 9-11, a group of teenagers explored such an alternative narrative in a dramatic arts program. We explored Jesus' nonviolent invitation through the stories and role-plays described above. Then the teens brainstormed various fictional characters that could have been involved in or touched by the tragedy, for example, a World Trade Center secretary, the daughter of a terrorist, an imagined terrorist himself. We developed several more fully by giving them a backstory — specific fears and hopes that motivated them, relationships and defining moments in their lives, and an understandable purpose driving their actions. We also identified who the enemy was for each character. I then asked each teen to write a short play portraying the challenges and possibilities of one or another character responding to their enemy with nonviolent love. For example, what would it look like for a U.S. citizen to love an Al Qaeda terrorist involved in a massive suicide bombing of a civilian population? Or vice versa? The following play was written by a seventeen-year-old Lutheran young lady who plays piano and loves to dance.

*Center stage looks like a hall for a wedding reception. An Arab man and an Anglo man are contentedly playing flute and violin toward the rear. A half-dozen couples, including children, are dancing on a dance floor. Others cluster around tables, chattering and enjoying the music.*

*From either end, two men are escorted onstage by two angels. The first is a Christian, Joseph, who is praising God that his years of faithfulness have led him to heaven upon his death. The second man is an Arab, Hakeem, praising Allah for his arrival in heaven as well. Joseph hears the music and remembers how he was once a promising violinist before giving up his music to become a businessman. He asks the angel if heaven might afford him the opportunity to play again. The angel shrugs, signaling "perhaps." Hakeem hears the music as well and remembers how much he loved to play flute as a child. He asks the angel if Allah might allow him to play once more, this time in Allah's court. The angel shrugs, "perhaps."*

*Joseph keeps strolling and expresses his excitement about being reunited with his dead daughter. The angel assures him that he will meet her soon.*

Hakeem likewise is eager to see his daughter, and is also assured of an imminent reception. Joseph becomes angry remembering how his daughter died at the hands of godless men during the World Trade Center attack. Hakeem becomes angry at how his daughter was killed by toxic poisoning from an oil plant under infidel control. The two shout in unison, "May the killers and their children and their children's children burn in hell forever. Praise be to Allah/Christ."

The angels stop and tell them that God is coming to greet them. Hakeem bows down awaiting Allah. He is surprised when he sees that Allah is a young Anglo girl. She welcomes him, then offers him one of the two flutes she is holding. Hakeem is delighted. He and the unconventional Allah play together with great joy. Across the stage, Joseph awaits the coming of Jesus with excitement. He is surprised to see that Jesus is a young Arab girl. She welcomes him and offers one of the two violins she is holding. He, too, is delighted to play with the unconventional Jesus.

With music, Allah and Jesus lead the two men to their dwelling place in heaven, a common table within the reception hall. As the two couples converge on the table, both men recognize their daughters with the other stranger. The daughters, delighted to see their fathers, drop their instruments, race into their father's arms, and are embraced with delight. The ballroom musicians keep playing as if serenading the reunion. The daughters lead their fathers by the hand toward the table the two will share. The men stop when they notice each other. Each of them asks what the other is doing there. "I refuse to share a home with that man," they both say.

"Yes," the daughters reply. "Hatred can turn even heaven into hell." Then they explain that the beauty of heaven is that the fathers get to live with their daughters, but only as the four live together, caring for one another as a family sitting around a common table.

The fathers are adamantly opposed and offended. Hakeem appeals to Allah. "How can you let this infidel into heaven?"

Allah turns to him and says, "The same way that I allow you." Hakeem is confused. "After all, I welcome you even after you killed me." Hakeem is aghast that he would ever kill his God. The young girl explains. "I was *one of the children in the World Trade Center that you attacked with your airplane." Hakeem is horrified.*

*Joseph is indignant. He appeals to Jesus demanding to know how Jesus can let such a terrorist into heaven. She responds, "The same way that I allow you." Joseph is confused. "I was one of the children that worked in your oil refinery in the Persian Gulf. I died of toxic poisoning because you didn't see the need for safety precautions." Joseph is horrified.*

*Joseph turns on Hakeem, asserting that at least he is not a cold-blooded killer. Hakeem turns on Joseph, disparaging the unsafe plant conditions, the capitalist greed that fuels American business, the imperialistic policies that killed his daughter and drove him into terrorism in the first place. The two scream at each other. They get louder and louder until simultaneously they slap each other in the face. The two ballroom musicians stop playing. The dancers stop dancing. All heaven goes silent. Allah and Jesus comfort the downcast musicians, then lead them to a table with food and drink. Then they look at their fathers. The two men are horrified that they have silenced the music of heaven. The girls come, take each of their hands, and lead them to the vacant musician chairs. They hand the two men a flute and violin. Hakeem and Joseph look at each other reluctantly. Jesus and Allah retrieve their own flute and violin and begin playing. Gradually, the fathers begin to play, then give themselves to the music. The dancers return to their dancing. The people return to their chattering.*

*Allah and Jesus quietly exit from opposite ends of the stage. The fathers continue to play. The dancers continue to dance. Two new strangers are escorted onstage from either side — a Palestinian and a Jew. Each carries a machine gun; each praises God to be in heaven after death; each expresses excitement at getting to see their dead daughters alive again. Which they will, the two angels affirm, any minute now.*

This play offers an alternative narrative to the myth of redemptive violence. It dares envision a heaven where Muslim, Jew, and Christian are all welcome. Both Christian businesspersons and Al Qaeda terrorists are complex human beings. They are capable of grief, love, and creative flourishing as well as of violence, self-deception, and complicity with evil acts. A complex web of international structures and practices contributes to violence even in its most harrowing forms. The "bad guy" is redeemable; the "good guy" has a shadow. Both are invited to participate in reconciled life, with the precondition that they help heal the violence to which they are partner.

The peacebuilding practice of loving our enemies beckons us to reflect on the narratives through which we determine good and evil, and by which we judge the relative redemptive powers of both violent and nonviolent responses to evil actions. We are invited to critique the insidious forms by which the myth of redemptive violence has a voice in our culture. And we are invited to offer a compelling alternative, to tell stories in which evil is met with nonviolent love, and all players are seen as complex and ambiguous human beings. Can we envision an Al Qaeda terrorist in heaven? Can we recognize our own ambiguous collusion with structures that create violence? Can we imagine a reconciliation where both victim and perpetrator are healed of the ways that violence lodges in the soul of us all, and where the spark that gives rise to the music within us as well is given the instrument to play and the space to flourish? Such are the possibilities that alternative narratives have to offer to the practice of Christian peacebuilding.

## "A DRUNK DRIVER'S DECISION": LOVING THE ENEMY THROUGH RESTORATIVE JUSTICE

Few of us know an Al Qaeda terrorist personally. Fewer of us still have insider knowledge regarding who will inhabit heaven and who will not. One of the purposes of an imaginary narrative such as the one above is to offer a symbolic frame through which to interpret real-life situations that persons or communities confront more regularly. In another dramatic arts program, a group of teens was invited to brainstorm scenarios where violent acts are more directly experienced.

Such situations included a community struggling with the presence of a convicted pedophile, a person whose car is stolen, and a woman being battered by her husband. Once again, we role-played and discussed Jesus' nonviolent invitation explored earlier in the chapter. Then we discussed the challenges and opportunities this invitation posed within the brainstormed scenarios. Several teens involved in peer mediation processes at their school enhanced the discussion with the principles of reparation and reconciliation those mediation processes assumed. I then asked the teens to write a play in small groups wrestling with responding to a perpetrator from one of their scenarios in appropriately loving ways. The following play was crafted by three driving-age teens.

*Scene one takes place at a high school party. Trent, a football star and world-class partyer, is drunkenly bragging about how well he can hold his liquor. Binge drinking while throwing a football at a butcher paper target, he is egged on by his inebriated buddies. The more he drinks, the louder his bravado, and the wilder his throws. When it is time to leave, his girlfriend begs him not to drive. The guys tease him, mocking both his apparent inability to hold liquor after all and the emasculating belittling by his lady. Trent erupts, grabs his keys, and storms off stage. "Watch this," he calls over his shoulder. The sound of squealing tires rips from offstage.*

*Scene two takes place in the living room of two grief-stricken parents. The mother mourns how her daughter was only thirteen years old, her whole life ahead of her. She can't believe her daughter was run over as she walked home from a friend's, the driver so drunk he left no skid marks when he hit her full speed. The father is beside himself with rage, wishing the driver had died in the crash as well, hoping that the monster will be sent to prison, enduring untold punishments, until he's a very old man. The mother cannot get over that the driver is just a teenager. The father is disgusted that the teen is no more than a self-centered jock who thinks he can do whatever he wants without consequence. Typical of a prima donna football star.*

*Scene three takes place in a courtroom. A judge finds the defendant, Trent, guilty of vehicular manslaughter. She listens to the parties as they appeal for the type of punishment Trent should suffer. The attorney for the parents argues that, given the egregious nature of the accident, the habitual pattern of the defendant's drinking, and the tragic loss that ensued, Trent should be sent to prison for the highest number of years allowed. The father makes a statement. His daughter is dead. For the rest of their lives, he and her mother will mark time by the proms the daughter will miss, the wedding that will not happen, the thriving career and the towheaded grandkids that will never materialize. A life has been lost. Nothing can bring it back. It is only just that Trent lose his as well, locked away and forced to live with the horror he brought into the world.*

*Trent's attorney argues that given the youth of the defendant, the tragic nature of his fatherless childhood, and the depth of his remorse, Trent should be placed on probation, his driver's license suspended, with the conditions that he attend an alcohol recovery program, refrain from drinking, and perform community service by volunteering for a junior high girl's sports program. Trent reads a statement. Every night he closes his eyes with the image of that girl in front of his car. He knows he can never bring her back. But he wants the parents to know that he will forever be sorry for what he did to all three of their lives.*

*The judge takes the matter under advisement.*

*Scene four takes place at Trent's home. The victim's parents knock on the door. With great effort, the father tells Trent how difficult it is to lose your only child. Trent listens with some understanding. The father rehearses the probation plan that Trent suggested to the court, then asks if Trent has found a sponsor for such a program. Trent says that he has yet to find one, but is diligently searching. The father tells Trent that part of him is consumed with hate toward Trent and wishes that Trent would be thrown into jail. He is grateful for a judge who takes so seriously the victim's needs for justice. But part of him wants to let go of such hatred. He tells Trent that he would be willing to recommend to the judge that she accept Trent's plan, and that he would volunteer to be Trent's sponsor. He will take Trent once a week to his recovery meetings and monitor his community service. He will keep Trent out of jail. On one condition. Every week that they drive to the meeting, they make one stop. At the grave of the daughter that Trent killed.*

*He gives Trent twenty-four hours to decide. If Trent agrees, he is to meet the father at the girl's grave the following afternoon.*

*Scene five takes place on a sidewalk the next day. Trent walks toward the side of the stage. From that direction, his partying friends walk toward him drinking beer and carousing loudly. When they see Trent, they bemoan, with stifled giggling, the tough break that befell Trent. Trent shrugs. They ask Trent where he is going. He tells them he is supposed to meet someone in a few minutes. The friends say that there is a great party getting started, Trent should come with them. Trent evasively demurs. They urge Trent to put the past behind him, and to make a comeback with his legendary drinking endurance. If nothing else, the party can help him forget about it all for a while. Trent hesitates. The friends coax. Trent says he'll think about it. The friends start walking off the stage telling him not to wimp out. Before they exit, they call a last time. "Here," one yells, pulling a beer out of brown paper bag. "It'll help you make your decision." He tosses the beer to Trent. The friends head off to the party.*

*Trent pauses center stage. He looks in the direction of his absent friends. He turns around and looks toward the unseen graveyard. Then, he studies the beer.*

*The lights go out.*

This play offers additional insights about the practice of loving one's enemy. Love is not sentimental. Egregious actions create deep wounds and those responsible for them should be held accountable. The story is honest about the understandable and natural feelings parents would have toward one who so negligently killed their child. An instinctive sense of justice cries out: an eye for an eye. Why should this football player's life thrive without consequence after so reprehensibly stealing another's in her youth? Throw the guy in jail and let the man rot.

This play, however, while acknowledging the very real feelings of rage and vindictiveness, offers an alternative response. The action taken is informed by understandings of restorative justice.[9]

Restorative justice is distinct from retributive justice. The latter metes out punishment for acts of wrongdoing. A person steals a car, she receives ten years in prison. Our current justice system is built on a sense of such retributive justice. The problems with such a system are several. Racial and economic inequities are built into the structures that dispense it. In addition, the convicted are offered little chance for rehabilitation, prisons more often intensifying violent propensities. Further, the victims, while assuaging a sense of justice, are denied an opportunity at healing or restitution. Restorative justice provides such an opportunity. It also offers a tough-love process through which one might practice nonviolence toward a wrongdoer.

When someone commits a violent act, that person should suffer consequences. These consequences need not be capricious nor vindictive. Root causes of the problem should be addressed — a drinking problem or a fatherless void, for example. In addition, the guilty party commits to reparations. While a life cannot be restored in the case of a killing, other actions can be performed — practices of grief and remembrance, a commitment to causes and projects that honor the victim and nurture life in others who might otherwise be disadvantaged. Responsibility and choice are placed in the hands of the victimizers. They person can follow a path that promises healing and some measure of redemption. Or they can simply suffer the retributive consequences of their actions.

The poignant ending of the play conceals this invitation. What will the boy choose, destructiveness or healing? While his path remains uncertain, that of the parents is not. They have chosen for healing. They have gone the extra mile to participate in the redemption of a victimizer. They have learned to let go of their need for vengeance. They are practicing a sober but transformative love for one who was their enemy.

# "A SOFTBALL BLOW-OUT": LOVING THE ENEMY THROUGH ENGAGING ONE'S SHADOW

The practice of loving our enemies is only truly possible when we face the enemy within ourselves. Walter Wink makes the audacious claim that our enemies are our greatest spiritual allies. Put succinctly, "The enemy can be the way to God."[10]

We all have people who push our buttons, people who repulse us, people whose behavior, politics, or impulses are reprehensible to us to the point of being untouchable. Depending on political or cultural persuasions, they may be people who are homosexual or homophobic, fundamentalist or libertarian, tree huggers or clear-cutting loggers, Iraqi terrorists or American warmongers. Some of our "enemies" emerge out of our personal constitutions — people who cut us off on the freeway perhaps, or are rude, or my son when he gives me that belligerent little smirk of his. These are people who trigger an instinctive revulsion within us as sure as a lightning bolt of aggression. Thank God we are *nothing* like such people.

Walter Wink suggests, thank God, yes. But not because we are so different. Because we are so similar.

People who trigger our antipathy embody repressed portions of our personal or collective shadows. They embody the untouchable parts of ourselves that we dread to admit are within us. Ashamed or un-comfortable with the sludgy parts of ourselves, we repress them from our consciousness, project them onto others, then reject such scape-goats with the vehemence of one whose life depends upon staying clean from such pollutedness. The spiritual gift of our enemies is that they reveal that evil which still resides in our own souls. With the clarity of a freshly polished mirror, they expose the violent impulses, the deep-seated wounds, or the unsatisfied yearnings that lie within ourselves. The invitation is to hold our own revulsions with compas-sion until the roots within ourselves are exposed and healed. Such action takes tenacious prayer, wise counselors, and a trust in the healing

Spirit to transform the material within our shadows into creative energy for good.[11]

In a creative writing workshop, a group of adults was asked to journal about a time in which somebody really set them off. Then they were invited to prayerfully hold both that person and themselves, asking God to dwell with the harsh energy in whatever way was appropriate to transform it into something life-giving. The following story is a paraphrase account of one such participant.

*I love to play softball. I love to shag fly balls, dive for grounders, smack line drives, and hump doubles into triples. I love the sport for the sheer play of it. I don't like to keep score, and I don't care who wins. I mean it when I say that I don't have a competitive bone in my body when it comes to softball. Ask my friends. I'm as easygoing as a gentle spring breeze on the grass at my feet.*

*But Mike is not. He's what you would call a first-class hothead. Mike slams into a catcher even if he can avoid it. He berates his teammates for errors, taunts opponents when they lose, and spews at umpires even if he's out by a mile. Quite frankly, I can't stand the guy nor the way he plays the game. I would never be like that. Not in a million years. I just like to enjoy the sport. He terrorizes everybody like a raging bull.*

*One day, an opposing team was one player short. I was afraid they would have to forfeit and we would have to go home. So I offered to play for the other team. After all, I don't care who wins anyway. Besides I still got to play left field.*

*The game became a titanic battle between two equally matched champions. We led by three, they caught up. They led by two, we caught up. Another rally and another lead change. Back and forth it went until we were ahead by two in the last inning. But Mike's team tied it up in the bottom half, so it was extra innings. We were all getting into it. Even the crowd. Players from the next game stood around and cheered each inning of the marathon. We scored twice in the tenth, Mike's team tied it up. Three more runs for us in the eleventh. Three more to tie up it for Mike. Every* lead was matched, every shutout was replicated. Thirteen innings, fourteen innings, all the way to the fifteenth inning. We went up by one. Mike's team came to bat. With one out, Mike ended up on third, another runner was on second, and I was out in left field.

And I knew exactly how Mike was going to play this. Any ball hit to the outfield for the second out, he was going to tag up and bolt home bowling through anybody in his way to score the tying run. Well, not on my watch. For once, I was going to put Mike in his place. I positioned myself an extra step back to be able to make a running catch on any ball for the momentum to snag Mike out at the plate. Sure enough, a soft line-drive was hit to left field. I lined it up in my sight. Mike was prepped at third. The catcher was shaking at home. I could just see it all happening, I was going to make a running catch, hurl a momentous strike to the plate, and Mike was going to be out on his butt.

The ball came. I lunged. I took a step, grabbed the ball, heaved to the plate. But wait a minute. Something was wrong. The ball was not in my mitt, it was not at my feet, it was not anywhere around me. In my haste, I had run completely by it. I turned and watched it bounding out toward the parking lot behind me, scooting obliviously away as not only Mike scored the tying run from third, but the runner on second scored the winning run as well for Mike and his team.

And I, the meek and noncompetitive guy who doesn't care who wins, I took my mitt, threw it to the ground, and verbally berated myself.

"How could you be so stupid," I seethed. "In front of God and everybody, you made a complete idiot of yourself." I fumed and kicked with such self-venom I couldn't settle down long enough to walk through the congratulatory walk. I stormed to my car and festered all the way home.

So I sat there in prayer, trying to hold both Mike and me with compassion, but still burning with shame at the tantrum I threw that was so uncharacteristic for me. And as I was watching myself in my imagination, standing in left field, storming around, something happened. I started swelling up like a balloon. It was weird. I was like an overinflated doll of myself getting bigger and bigger, a ballooning giant of myself, until I was a huge Macy's

*Thanksgiving Parade float of myself, still swelling bigger and bigger, then finally exploding. Balloon fragments of me blew all over the field. And all that was left, like the elderly professor behind the curtain of the almighty Oz, was a little runt of a boy all of seven years old. It was me, when I was a kid relegated to right field in Little League because I was so bad, praying to God that nobody would hit the ball to me because I couldn't stand the humiliation of dropping it. And the little boy of myself looked up at the adult me and said, "Why do you hate me so much?"*

*And I realized he was right. I can't stand people who belittle others for not playing well. I can't stand them because I am just like them. I don't do it to others. I do it to myself. I still hate the boy in me who has a hard time just catching the ball and aches for somebody to think he's a star anyway.*

Goethe once remarked that the height of human wisdom is the knowledge that there is no evil action within the world that is not within oneself as well. Herman Melville said it another way. "We're all sharks. Angels are just sharks well governed."[12] It is all too easy to dismiss those we detest as being beneath our dignity. The hard truth is that those we most detest are those we most resemble. They may symbolize fantasies we are loath to admit, impulses we cannot own, or wounds that have yet to heal. But in one form or another, the evil we see in others is within ourselves as well. And a truly compassionate attitude is only possible when we encounter and reconcile with the evil that lies within.

Loving our enemies is an agonizingly challenging practice of Christian peacebuilding. Practicing it is messy, complex, and both socially and psychologically threatening. But so much is at stake that we must try. Erich Neumann observes that one can go to war with another only when that one has been converted into a bearer of our own shadow.[13] In a time when war is being waged, such an observation is truly sobering. Jesus invites us to pray for our enemies. May we indeed find that source of grace that enables us to hold with compassion the enemies around us, the baseball hotheads, the killing drunk drivers, even the Al Qaeda terrorists — both those in our world and those within ourselves.

## NOTES

1. Walter Wink, *Engaging the Powers* (Minneapolis: Fortress Press, 1992), 263.

2. For a variation on this tale, see Ed Brody et al., *Spinning Tales, Weaving Hope* (Philadelphia: New Society Publishers, 1992), 137–39.

3. The following analysis is dependent upon Walter Wink. For this and a brilliant interpretation of Jesus' other two nonviolent examples, going the extra mile and surrendering one's tunic when only a coat is demanded, see Wink, *Engaging the Powers*, 175–84.

4. Ibid., 177.

5. Ibid., 265.

6. The pieces are offered with permission under the condition of anonymity.

7. David Polkinghorne, *Narrative Knowing and the Human Sciences* (Albany: State University of New York Press, 1988), 1.

8. Wink, *Engaging the Powers*, 13.

9. For a primer on restorative justice, see Howard Zehr, *The Little Book of Restorative Justice* (Intercourse, Pa.: Good Books, 2002).

10. Wink, *Engaging the Powers*, 273.

11. For excellent resources in praying with one's shadow material, see Robert Johnson, *Inner Work: Using Dreams and the Active Imagination for Personal Growth* (San Francisco: HarperCollins, 1986), and Morton Kelsey, *The Other Side of Silence: Meditation for the Twenty-First Century* (Mahwah, N.J.: Paulist Press, 1995).

12. Paraphrased from Herman Melville, *Moby Dick, Or the Whale* (New York: W. W. Norton, 1976), 294.

13. Erich Neumann, *Depth Psychology and a New Ethic*, trans. Eugene Rolfe (New York: G. P. Putnam & Sons, 1969), 57.

# CHAPTER FIVE

# BETWEEN ADVOCACY AND DIALOGUE

## Peacebuilding in the Classroom

*Carol Lakey Hess*

*We teach to change the world.* — Stephen D. Brookfield

*The classroom remains the most radical space of possibility in the academy.* — bell hooks

I agree with bell hooks: classrooms are radical places for the possibility of peacemaking.[1] Not just classrooms in the academy, but any space where teaching and learning are taking place. The possibility of peacemaking in the classroom, however, is complicated. It carries within it an inherent tension — the tension between a peacemaking position and a peacemaking process, or what I call the tension between advocacy and dialogue. It is this tension that I would like to address in this chapter. I begin with a classroom illustration.

When I started work on this essay, the United States was at war with Iraq. On April 5, 2003, the *New York Times* online included an article, "With Current War, Professors Protest, as Students Debate." The article focuses on Amherst College but notes that many campuses face the tension between more liberal, antiwar faculty and a more conservative, Reagan era–raised student body. The *Times* online front-paged the following quote by an Amherst College sophomore: "It seems the professors are more vehement than the students. There comes a point when you wonder are you fostering a discussion or are you promoting an opinion you want students to embrace or even parrot?"

In the body of the article, the writer notes: "Here at Amherst College, many students were vocally annoyed this semester when forty professors paraded into the dining hall with antiwar signs. One student confronted a protesting professor and shoved him."

The article ends with the following:

At Amherst, Prof. Barry O'Connell, too, tries hard. As he sits in a discussion group with students, he patiently listens to those who argue in favor of the war, even though he remains adamantly against it. Across the hall, a mug shot of Henry A. Kissinger is posted outside his office with the heading "Wanted for Crimes Against Humanity." "My job is not to get my students to agree with me," Professor O'Connell insisted. Still, he conceded, "There is a second when I hear them, and my heart just falls."

These scenarios give a glimpse into how complicated it is to navigate between advocacy and dialogue. Advocacy focuses more on vision; it is the articulation of a clear standpoint. Dialogue, however, focuses more on process; it is the fostering of community interaction. To be more precise, I define "advocacy" as: "the presenting of a position and providing reasons that others should adopt it."[2] Borrowing from Stephen Brookfield's description of "democratic discourse," I define "dialogue" as "the ability to talk and listen respectfully to those who hold views different from our own." Furthermore, I agree with Stephen Brookfield that dialogue "is a habit that is rarely learned or practiced in daily life."[3] While I argue later that advocacy and dialogue, vision and process, are not absolute distinctions, they do have different emphases.

With these definitions in mind, consider the difficult yet important position teachers are in with regard to an issue like the war in Iraq. On the one hand, if we teachers who care about peace and justice advocate so strongly that we leave students feeling that they must "parrot" our viewpoint, we have advocated for peace in a way that compromises peacebuilding processes. On the other hand, if we professors merely sit, listen, and let our "heart just fall," we have created a process that leads us to tolerate injustice without standing up for justice. In the former, we run the risk of doing violence to others; in the latter, we run the risk of permitting the violence of others to prevail.

As I understand it, peace (shalom) includes both the absence of violence and the presence of well-being and justice. Peace is *not* the same as harmony, if harmony is understood as the avoidance of conflict. In fact, peacemaking classrooms are often hard places to be — at least at first. Peacemaking classrooms are places where differences are neither ignored nor squelched; they are engaged. Such classrooms make a high demand on participants. I find helpful Ellen Ott Marshall's use of the term "peacebuilding." This is what the classroom can contribute to world peace: a space for the building of nonviolent means (dialogue) to develop and promote our visions of well-being (advocacy). In classrooms, we can learn and practice — build — habits that have implications beyond the classroom. More than that, we can build habits in relatively safe environments *before* people face issues where life and death are at stake.

## A SPIRITUALITY FOR INNER AND OUTER DIVERSITY

In order to engage the diversity outside of us, we do well to face and engage the diversity inside of us. Carl Jung observed that the "present day shows with appalling clarity how little able people are to let the other [person's] argument count, although this capacity is a fundamental and indispensable condition for any human community." Jung went on to say:

> Everyone who proposes to come to terms with himself must reckon with this basic problem. For, to the degree that he does not admit the validity of the other person, he denies the "other" within himself the right to exist — and vice versa. *The capacity for inner dialogue is a touchstone for outer objectivity.*[4]

We all have within us experiences, feelings, and potentials that range along the entire spectrum of the issues for which we take passionate, coherent, and articulated stands. Or, to put it another way, even those who advocate for peace and diversity have within us violence and a preference for our own kind. If we teachers face, and admit to, our own participation in a tendency toward violence, we will be less arrogant and more compassionate in our advocating.

Those of us who are committed to peacemaking need to come to terms with our experiences of injustice, our anger at those experiences, and the part of us that is violent enough to want to fight, go to war, even kill someone. If we haven't personally experienced an injustice so deep that we have this kind of anger, we need to spend some time with a person or community who has. We cannot understand peacemaking if we have not felt driven to war by the rage of injustice. Moreover, we cannot understand, or argue with, the traditions of those (including our forebears) that emerged during periods of oppression and injustice if we do not understand these often suppressed aspects within ourselves.

In addition to facing our inner violence, we also need to face our inner will to control. There is both beauty and danger to passion. It is our passion for peace and justice that energizes our hard work on behalf of these. It is also our passion for peace and justice that makes us impatient with slow and halting means toward peace and justice. When we think we are right, we are susceptible to wanting to enforce our rightness. While we do need to set rules and enforce laws aimed at peace and justice, we also need to continually grapple with the threshold between healthy boundaries and rigid will-to-control. When we cannot resolve the tension, we need to honestly name that it exists and thoughtfully consider when a threshold has been crossed.

When we who work for peace fail to see the rage and violence and the will-to-control within us, we deceive ourselves into thinking that the rage and violence in the world belongs only to those who are "other" to us. We "split" that part of ourselves off from our consciousness and see it only in others.[5] This comes from a fear of seeing the ambiguity and imperfection in our selves, our commitments, our traditions. Truth is, health comes not from repressing these aspects, but from facing and understanding them.

Recently, I assigned a group of students to lead a Bible study on the Syrophoenician woman of Mark 7:24–30 — a passage rife with ambiguity. I was quite familiar with this passage (and I admit I had my hopes for what it would bring to our class discussions). When the class members who were leading this study asked the other class members to name those who today might be considered and called "dogs" (see Mark 7:28), I was taken aback by the responses. Until that moment, I was set to put myself on the side of the woman and her oppressed company; many in the class, however, named soldiers fighting in Iraq as contemporary dogs. These were not exactly the "dogs" I was poised to love. I wanted different "dogs" upon which to show my compassion and righteousness. While I myself have been careful to avoid bad-mouthing soldiers, I realized that many on "my side" of the issue were perceived as having dehumanized those who supported or believed in this war. I was stunned into inner dialogue. I not only had a Canaanite woman within, I had an angry, name-calling dehumanizer within as well.

Thus, the "outward work" of justice seeking and peacebuilding requires parallel, prior inner work. The words of the mystic Meister Eckhart are helpful here:

> The outward work
> will never be puny
> if the inward work
> is great.
> And the outward work
> can never be great or even good
> if the inward one is puny or of little worth.
> The inward work invariably
> Includes in itself
> all expansiveness,
> all breadth,
> all length,
> all depth.
> Such a work
> receives and draws all its being
> from nowhere else except
> from and in the heart of God.[6]

A teacher who has done such inner work has not resolved life's ambiguities! A teacher who has done inner work, however, is in a healthier place to grapple with the tension between dialogue and advocacy in the classroom — and it is to this classroom tension that we now return.

I first look here at the dynamics of dialogue, and then turn to advocacy. The skill of dialogue I earlier defined as the ability to talk and listen respectfully to those who hold views different from our own. Here I consider two basic forms of dialogue: fair debate and enlargement of issue discussions.

## PEACEBUILDING DIALOGUE

Whenever I teach classes, I begin with an invitation to genuine dialogue. In doing so, I also point to the dangers of "Groupthink." In *Joining Together*, David and Frank Johnson include a description of

Groupthink, "the collective striving for unanimity that overrides group members' motivation realistically to appraise alternative courses of action." Groupthink censors disagreement and thereby diminishes reality testing and moral judgment because it ignores information inconsistent with the favored view or course of action. "Groupthink leads to concurrence seeking — group members inhibit discussion in order to avoid any disagreement or arguments, emphasize agreement, and avoid realistic appraisal of alternative ideas and courses of action."[7]

Teaching the skills of fair debate and then using them is one way to avoid Groupthink. The strategy of debate could be either a method for advocating (because each participant does advocate) or a method of dialogue. I start this section on dialogue with a discussion of fair debate because I think debate, respectfully done, is one way to harness advocates toward a disciplined conversation. The careful presentation of more than one viewpoint, and the subsequent probing and questioning of those viewpoints, is the *sine qua non* of both dialogue and debate. Although I do not think debate is always the best way to engage controversy, I think it can be useful. In order for debate to be a "peacebuilding" process, *disciplined* listening and *fair* feedback are needed. I typically use this process for groups rather than individuals, so that the positions are developed with the participation of many voices.

### Fair Debate

Johnson and Johnson invoke John Stuart Mill (to whom we return below) as they start their chapter on "Controversy and Creativity." Mill stated: "Since the general or prevailing opinion on any subject is rarely or never the whole truth, it is only by the collision of adverse opinion that the remainder of the truth has any chance of being supplied."[8]

Here is the process I teach.

- List the key arguments of your position.
- Take turns presenting arguments.

- Listen to and record with fairness the arguments of the other group (who will be given the chance to hold you accountable to your description).

- Name two insights the other group has raised that have expanded your understanding of the issue.

- List two questions you have for the other group.

- Write responses you have to the other group's arguments.

- Write responses to the other group's questions.

- List possible "third ways" of looking at or responding to the issue.

- Name the places where you perceive clear, and currently irreconcilable, differences between your perspective and that of others.

I have used this debate format in a variety of ways, and I'll describe three of them. (1) Several years ago, when many of our mainline denominations produced new, more contemporary, and more inclusive hymnals, I used this for groups discussing or debating whether or not the church should purchase new hymnals. (2) When I was teaching a session on Psalm 137 (read the psalm in its entirety if you do not know its content), we addressed the tough issues this Psalm provokes. I divided the class into two groups with the following assignment: Imagine you are a "canonization committee" appointed to reconsider what should be included in the Bible. Would you include Psalm 137? What are the gifts and the burdens of this Psalm?[9] (3) In several places, where communities were grappling with the issue of whether or not homosexuality was part of the goodness of God's plan for creation, I used this format to give a platform to opposing theological arguments. (It is important for me to note here that debate formats do not work well if a community is in a situation of high conflict; in those instances, more sophisticated mediation techniques are necessary.)

While I use debate formats from time to time, I am aware of gender and culture studies which alert teachers to the fact that debate originated in — and continues to be more comfortable for — the education of elite males.[10] Furthermore, Deborah Tannen has recently critiqued the contentious cultural climate that the rhetoric of debate has created.[11] Therefore, I also use other forms of discourse that promote an "enlargement of the issue" with a more collaborative form. I suggest here two forms of issue enlargement: "barn raising" and "diversifying."

### Enlargement of Issue Discussion

In her book *Argument Culture*, Deborah Tannen argues that there are other ways to deal with controversial issues than adversarial debate. Tannen retains a commitment to public argument, but she wants to temper the adversarial hostility — and its attendant disregard for truth — that has corrupted argument.

According to Tannen, one of the major problems with the debate model of dealing with difficult issues is that it leaves the impression that there are just two sides. If we imagine there are only two sides then we do not explore the complexities of the issue — and neither do we give space for views that are not quite either/or. "Instead of asking 'What's the other side?,'" suggests Tannen, "we might ask instead, 'What are other sides?' Instead of insisting on hearing 'both sides,' we might insist on hearing 'all sides.'" Tannen also suggests that we expand our notion of debate to include more dialogue. "In dialogue, each statement that one person makes is qualified by a statement made by someone else, until the series of statements and qualifications moves everyone closer to a fuller truth." That doesn't mean there isn't argument. "In dialogue, there is opposition, yes, but no head-on collision. Smashing heads does not open minds."[12]

Although sometimes we need to join with those who believe similarly in order to work for justice, we also need to be cautious about creating an assumption that there is an "us," and there is a "them," and that the two are neat and discrete categories. Many issues lead to multiple perspectives. I once had a conversation with a person regarding the issue of whether or not homosexual love could be understood as part of God's good intentions for creation. I mentioned monogamous gay relationships, and my conversation partner said: "It never occurred to me when thinking about this issue that this could be a variant of what it means to be homosexual." While I myself came to the issue from the other side — the first gay persons I got to know well (both women and men) were in committed relationships — this person had been influenced by an understanding that considered homosexuality and monogamy antithetical. The unraveling of this completely changed the "debate" for her. There was no longer an "us" and a "them" but a third group of people who accepted gay relationships but held them accountable to conventional patterns of fidelity.

What if our goal, when facing difficult issues, were not to argue or persuade, but rather to gather, listen, expand? What if, rather than lay out the opposing sides of an issue, we explored the spectrum of positions?

Now, of course, there are limits to diversifying. Peacebuilding processes of dialogue alone do not ensure the fullness of well-being. As I noted above, a commitment to peacebuilding dialogue can lead teachers to empower and include viewpoints whose content is not geared to peacebuilding. For instance, my feminist commitment to the rights of women is sometimes in conflict with my desire to listen to other groups of people. When dealing with issues that impact justice toward women, how far should I go in diversifying perspectives? Susan Moller Okin (the late political scientist at Stanford University) raised this issue in her essay "Is Multiculturalism Bad for Women?"[13] Okin argued that when the dominant ideas and practices of a group work against the Western liberal idea that men and women are moral equals, we ought, especially in matters pertaining to law (her expertise), to be less solicitous of the group and more attentive to the costs visited on women. In other words, Okin asserted that cultural tolerance ought not be accepted when it is used as an excuse for gender injustice. As a feminist committed to multiculturalism and religious pluralism, my advocacy stand and my commitment to dialogue keep me in a continual state of negotiation and reflection. I return to this issue below.

Now, as I suggested earlier, an absolute dichotomy between advocacy and dialogue, the content and the process of peacemaking, is false. A teacher can't help but shape others. Stephen Brookfield, an educator influenced by critical social theory, puts it well: "If you don't want to influence what people think and do, then you shouldn't teach and you definitely shouldn't write books about teaching."[14] Thus, we can't pretend to teach apolitically, neutrally, or without some form of advocacy. Truth is, the very act of setting up peacebuilding processes itself is an advocacy for peacebuilding processes. And, on the other side, as we shall soon see, advocacy itself can be done in a dialogical manner.

Amitai Etzioni raises another issue with regard to the relationship between the *process* and the *outcome* of dialogue. He argues that dialogue itself cannot justify a decision.[15] He imagines, for instance, that a fascist conference would still discourse toward fascist conclusions, even if there were "dialogue" taking place involving difference. The "sides of a debate" and the bounds of the "enlargement" are only as open as the gathered group allows. Thus, Iris Young, political philosopher at the University of Chicago, argues that democracies should always be regional and not merely local, because local interests can be provincial and undemocratic vis-à-vis the larger society.[16]

We could argue that dialogue, if constituted by the right proportions of diverse people, disciplined by the right processes, and checked for power issues, would not lead to fascist or undemocratic solutions. To a certain degree, I think this is true. That is to say, I advocate for fair fighting. Still, I am also aware that it might require near-fascist vigilance to ensure a perfectly fair process! And here I have perhaps reached a limit or a boundary to dialogue, a boundary beyond which I cannot go. So now, I turn to the other side of the tension — the side of advocacy. Here I describe ways in which I believe advocacy can, on the one hand make its stand, while on the other hand check its will-to-control and contribute to peacebuilding.

## PEACEBUILDING ADVOCACY

I have defined advocacy as "the presenting of a position and providing reasons that others should adopt it." Teachers, as I have already admitted, unavoidably advocate. Or, to use the direct language that Stephen Brookfield uses: we teach to change the world. I would add: otherwise, why bother? I am a teacher because I'm not happy with the way things are in this world and I think I can make a difference through education. That being said, I still think there are ways to advocate that are faithful to one's passion and respectful of and empowering toward others.

I suggest here three approaches to peacebuilding advocacy: enlarging our passions, dynamic traditioning, and dialogue *even when we know we are right*.

### Enlarging Passions

The worst position for a student to be in, according to Stephen Brookfield, is to sense that a teacher has an agenda and a preferred way of working, but to not be told what the operating values are. Students feel that if they do not have this information, they cannot trust the teacher or understand the class dynamics.[17] This also places at an advantage those who know, or can figure out, what the teacher's stances or values are — leading to an unjust distribution of knowledge and power. Thus, a well-intentioned, but politically naive, commitment to "neutrality" in the classroom can sabotage the attempt to build peace through dialogue.

Peacebuilding advocacy often fosters more participation and a greater sense of well-being than the pretense of neutrality. When a teacher exposes his or her own location and passions, he or she reduces any anxiety caused by class participants not knowing where he or she is coming from. To pretend that passions and agendas don't exist only allows these passions to either emerge surreptitiously or remain submerged confusingly. Furthermore, to withhold revealing our commitments communicates that they must not be exposed to critique. This can also lead to a mystification of our position — an aura that intensifies anxiety. A critically reflective teacher who makes her own thinking public and subject to critical discussion actually promotes both the content and the process of peacebuilding discourse.

For instance, in a course I teach on Teaching the Bible as Liberating Word, I name myself a feminist. In that course, we look at issues of sexism, racism, colonialism, and anti-Judaism in Christian history and tradition, but I address these issues in terms of the ways feminists have both named *and participated in* these oppressions. More than that, I address the ways in which even we who face society's biases still are part of a *system of advantage* that favors some over others (for example, white women over women of color).[18] Even we who claim to have no negative prejudice must look at a system that privileges some over others. There is no purified "us" and "them" when it comes to these oppressions, and even those who take liberational stands must be continually self-critical about their participation in oppression.

I find Carol Christ's model for scholarship a helpful way to describe a peacebuilding process of advocacy. Acknowledging that researchers bring to their work a passion for something particular as well as a willingness to learn from voices which stretch and modify that passion, Christ poses three "moments" for scholarship: (1) naming the passion, (2) enlarging the perspective, and (3) exercising judgment.[19] The first moment involves an awareness and articulation of the scholar's position and the passion for transformation that drives her work. The second moment is to enlarge the position by further study and openness to differing viewpoints. The third moment involves a return to the now-expanded standpoint, incorporating the insights gained. We can say that these are also three moments for advocacy: naming our passion, enlarging our perspective, and exercising judgment in expanding our viewpoint.

I think it is also important for teachers who wish to advocate to openly show how they come to their views. All positions are the result of struggle, and all positions still have unresolved tensions and problems. There's a deep honesty to naming this. Advocates who wish to be fair and invested in peacebuilding can recognize and name the limitations of their views; they can demonstrate self-critique, and they can open their views to the critiques of others.[20] Likewise, teachers who advocate can take care not to oversimplify the views of those who differ and not to argue in a way that dehumanizes others. As I name my passion in teaching and writing, I need to use the kind of criteria of fairness toward the works of others with whom I disagree as I ask others to use in my classroom debates. When care is taken to advocate our passion with honesty and respect, both the content and process of peacebuilding is honored.

### Dynamic Traditioning: "Questioning and Wrestling"

The practice of passing on a tradition is a kind of advocacy. We share a tradition because we have passion for its history, stories, commitments, and vision. Unfortunately, traditions become vulnerable to what Jarislav Pelikan called "traditionalism," a static and rigid understanding of the faith of those who came before us that can lead to closedness and injustice. Yet, the traditioning process itself can be a dynamic interaction between advocacy and dialogue. Alasdair MacIntyre describes a "living tradition" as "an historically extended, socially embodied argument, and an argument precisely in part about the goods which constitute a tradition."[21]

The capacity to sustain diversity, tension, and conflict in the classroom is needed for healthy traditioning processes. It is my view that one of the best ways to conduct a "traditioning" process is to focus on the enduring questions of a tradition, with an awareness that the answers are often contextual and provisional. In this way, traditioning, rather than being a "Q and A" (questioning and answering), becomes a "Q and W" — a questioning and wrestling with what has come before us for our interpretation and reconstruction.[22] The Christian tradition asks deep, rich, and poignant questions: Why is there evil? Why do some people suffer? Where is God in the midst of suffering? Does God care about oppression? Is there order to the universe? Is there justice in the universe? How long? The Christian tradition includes a multiplicity of answers, some of which are promising, some of which are dissatisfying, all of which are partial and mixed with human fallibility.

Biblical scholar Katheryn Pfisterer Darr argues that it is important for communities of faith to grapple with difficult texts in the tradition. "Sometimes we continue to embrace hurtful texts not because we affirm their answers, but rather because they force us to confront the important questions."[23] We do not have any traditions, including biblical traditions, that are not carried in fallible, partial vessels. We have rich, earthy, ambiguous, pain-imbued, sometimes pain-inflicting traditions wrought in passion. In asking and reasking the questions, and in wrestling with the groping answers to the questions, we gain wisdom — even if not certainty.

### Dialogue When We Know We Are Right

Nancy Duff writes that a moral dilemma arises "either when one discovers equally plausible (but mutually exclusive) alternatives to a moral issue or when one finds no adequate solution at all to an issue."[24] People are more open to listening to opposing points of view when they sense this kind of dilemma. Contrariwise, once people are certain of their position, they are no longer in a dilemma, and they are less likely to listen to opposing viewpoints.

There are some controversial issues that pose no moral dilemma for us — that is to say, we know where we stand on them, and we realize that we are not likely to have our position changed by hearing arguments from another side. For instance, as with Duff, I stand with those for whom homosexuality is not a moral dilemma, I uphold the ordination of homosexual persons, and I believe that faithful and monogamous gay unions are consistent with the will of God.

I am a member of a denomination, however, that battles over this issue, and when it comes to live battles within our communities, Duff suggests we remain open to hearing opposing views. Drawing on John Stuart Mill's essay "On Liberty," she advises those of us who are convinced of the goodness of our beliefs and positions not to turn away from debate or disregard the value of opposing positions.[25] Duff summarizes the three reasons Mill gives for this:

*a.* "Because we are fallible, if we silence an opposing opinion we may be silencing the truth." Below I argue that there are some boundaries as to what we allow into debates and conversations. But, in making this point, Mill was urging that we avoid simply asserting the truth of our position to close down conversation. We should hone and test our position through thoughtful processes, and we should realize that our position is bound to have flaws and limitations. This leads to Mill's second point.

*b.* "Even if the opposing opinion is clearly in error, it may contain a portion of the truth." I take this to mean that we may still have something to learn from hearing why the group with the opposing view holds that view, which may expand our understanding of the issue. This point can be deepened further if we enlist here one of Amitai Etzioni's "rules of engagement" for values talks between conflicting parties in the same community (but this would also hold between communities). Etzioni urges that contesting parties should avoid "demonizing" one another; "they should refrain from depicting the other side's values as completely negative, as when they are characterized as 'satanic.' "[26]

In her recent book *Divinity and Diversity*, which is a theological affirmation of religious pluralism, Marjorie Suchocki gives theological weight to this call to avoid demonizing.[27] As a feminist, she describes how she sustains her commitment to inclusivity toward women while also holding open conversation with those who do not hold this commitment. The gospel, she argues:

> calls me to refrain from demonizing this one with whom I ardently disagree. To the contrary, I am called to listen even as I speak. I might even hear the other ask what the church is doing to

alleviate the condition of the strangers within America's gates, for the same criterion I hold relative to the other is one I must apply to Christianity.[28]

Suchocki is clear that dialogue does not require the suspension of important values. To the contrary, dialogue requires honest offering of ourselves. This also means, however, that when we name a value, we open ourselves to new revelations of how we continue to commit the wrongs we name in others. I will never forget the time I heard a Muslim woman ask: Why is it that Western women think that a burka is more oppressive than miniskirts and high heels? Now, it is true that many Western feminists have spoken out against the culture that promotes miniskirts and high heels. It is also true that some Muslim women themselves find burkas oppressive. Still, there is revelatory value in this woman's comment, and I paused to consider where there may be many logs in our Western Christian eyes when we point to the splinters in the eyes of our sisters and brothers.

I would add a corollary to this call to avoid demonizing: we should not announce that our view or side is God's view or side. We can fairly argue that we believe our view is most consistent with the impulse of our faith tradition, or we can argue that our view is the result of faithful religious questioning and struggle. But, when it comes to naming God's position — if such language is even fitting — I doubt any of us has a sufficiently complex view of things to come anywhere close to staking that claim. In fact, I once did not sign a petition with which I agreed because it began, "In the name of God." There are some religious traditions that are wary of even speaking the name of God, and I think we need to at least be wary of invoking the name of God for our position.

c. "Even if the opinion we hold is the whole truth, it risks becoming no more than prejudice or recitation if it refuses to be in conversation with other opinions." Although I doubt any of us thinks we have the whole truth, we may think we are mostly right about certain things and don't need to keep thinking about them. I address some boundary situations below, but in many cases we do need to keep our "right opinions" fresh and renewable. For instance, although I doubt I will ever stop being a feminist, I have learned from critics of feminism that there are some issues that we have ignored (especially the needs of poor women) that need to be addressed.

I have found these three points from Mill to be valuable in my own moral reflection, and I would like to add two more.

d. If we shut down dialogue, we shut down dissent, and we begin to create a homogenous community that avoids conflict. Sometimes it seems to me that debates over controversial issues lead to each side creating a "sheep and goats" mentality that subtly suggests or even invokes a desire that all goats be corralled and controlled. This promotes the kind of Groupthink I named earlier.

Communities can become vulnerable to fear of dissent and promotion of homogeneity. Political philosopher Iris Young argues that the "ideal of community" that many of us hold prefers homogeneity and operates to either assimilate or exclude those who are different. In the yearning for harmony, sameness becomes the primary value in the ideal of community, and difference and dissent are treated almost like betrayal. This can happen even in communities of people that join together to advocate justice for particular groups. Young warns, "If in their zeal to affirm a positive meaning of group specificity people seek or try to enforce a strong sense of mutual identification, they are likely to reproduce exclusions similar to those they confront."[29]

e. Finally, if we stop talking to those with opposing viewpoints, we project an "otherness" onto those with whom we disagree and fail to see the "otherness" in ourselves. For instance, if I, a feminist, keep insisting that patriarchy and sexism are "out there," I do not see how it is also "in here." Yes, I do, sometimes very conspicuously, *stand* with those who believe in and work toward the flourishing of all women, but as did most of us, I grew up in patriarchal soil. In fact, Marjorie Suchocki revisits the doctrine of "original sin" as that "which precedes us bending us willy-nilly against inclusive good."[30] Even as I fight domination of women by elite men, I also must see the part of me that dominates others. Our world is not divided into sexists and nonsexists. Perhaps we feminists, antiracists, and other liberation-oriented folk ought to borrow from Alcoholics Anonymous and name ourselves to be "in recovery." We have all imbibed sexism and racism, and if we do not name this, we are in denial. Even those of us who feel we are free from prejudice need to name the systems of advantage from which we benefit (systems that privilege some over others). As feminists have been called to task for inadvertent racism and white privilege, anti-Judaism, and colonialism, we all continually need to face in ourselves that which we fight outside ourselves.

Clearly, these points are not meant to prevent us from making decisions. These are habits to cultivate *in the midst of* advocacy and decisions.

There's a wonderfully paradoxical dialogue in Anne Tyler's *St. Maybe*: the story of Ian, a teenaged boy who feels guilty for the death of his brother and atones for it by joining the offbeat Church of the Second Chance and devoting his life to raising his brother's stepchildren. Ian's father and the father of another church member attend a church picnic. Scornfully referring to the church as The Church of the Second Rate, the other father asks Ian's father: "Want to hear what I hate most about churches? They think they know the answers. I really hate that. It's the people who *don't* know the answers who are going to heaven, I tell you." To which his daughter, a fierce devotee of this church, replies, "But the minute you say that, you see, you yourself become a person who knows the answers."

We who wish to advocate for peace and justice are caught in a paradox. We feel passionately about our stances, and yet we know we need to guard against absolutizing those stances. As soon as we know who's going to heaven and who's not, we get dangerously close to becoming violent.

Now the question arises: how far can we extend the logic of diversity? Every person and group must draw boundaries, and a commitment to diversity doesn't abolish boundaries. In any setting, for practical as well as moral reasons, some things are let in and others are not. Groups committed to diversity try to expand the board of people that makes boundary decisions; they toil with great care to be more just than not, but at the end of the day there are boundaries.

Significantly, Deborah Tannen points out in *The Argument Culture* that the current tendency to polarize every issue, to assume that there is always an opposition between two sides, sometimes prompts people to give a platform to "kooks who state outright falsehoods." She particularly points to the way in which Holocaust deniers have been successful in gaining television and newspaper coverage by masquerading as "the other side" in a "debate." Continual reference to the other side results in a pervasive conviction that everything has another side — and that that other side always deserves as much consideration. While all issues have multiple facets, we do need to draw boundaries when it comes to lining up positions. Some things — for instance, the wrongful North American enslavement of African people; the wrongful genocide of Native American people; the wrongful Nazi murders of Jews, gypsies, gays, political dissidents, and disabled people; the wrongful subordination of women to men — these do not belong on a debate platform. Surely, there are multiple facets to the issues, and those can be discussed, but in my view these are the kinds of places that a boundary must be named.

Even so, boundaries are always controversial, contested, provisional, and even somewhat permeable. My own boundaries, particularly when it comes to women, are continually tested and stretched. Anyone who has been involved with ecumenical groups knows how excruciating it is to define boundaries. To require, for instance, that all groups welcome the ordination of women excludes many; yet to include those that exclude women seems like a compromise with injustice. We can't avoid the arduous task of naming boundaries and thus excluding, and we can't avoid the excruciating pain of finding that some of our deepest core principles come into conflict with one another. As Brookfield notes, "attempts to increase the amount of love and justice in the world are never simple, never unambiguous."[31]

Whenever we draw boundaries or even come to the point of exclusions — for instance, we may not invite a member of the KKK to speak at a forum on civil rights — we should still know about the group we are excluding. For instance, the Southern Poverty Law Center a few years back published a sensitive essay on why hate groups are attracting underclass youth. About the same time, the *Philadelphia Inquirer* had a front-page article entitled "The Politics of Xenophobia kindled in W. Europe." The recent wave of xenophobia, fear of the other, in countries like Austria and Switzerland, as the newspapers tell it, is not simply bald hate, but is linked to employment and crime issues. If we don't understand the larger contexts in which hate is fueled, we fail to see that we all contribute in one way or another to the very injustices we wish to fight.

And, as we have already seen, we get away with splitting evil from ourselves and projecting it all onto others. If we project all, or most, racism onto the KKK, we fail to see the more subtle and possibly more potent expressions of it in our midst.

•

I opened with a quote from bell hooks: "The classroom remains the most radical space of possibility in the academy." I would like to close with more of hooks's hard-won educational wisdom. In the midst of a discussion on teaching, hooks warns that critically reflective classrooms that embrace dialogue and diversity will face "much more tension" than other classrooms. Tension can be uncomfortable both for teachers and students who think that harmony is a sign of successful teaching. "The exciting aspect of creating a classroom community where there is respect for individual voices is that there is infinitely more feedback because students do feel free to talk — and talk back. And, yes, often this feedback is critical," hooks states. She goes on, "moving away from the need for immediate affirmation was crucial to my growth as a teacher."[32] Furthermore, hooks reveals that she learned to "respect the pain" that students go through when they encounter those whose experiences pose challenges to their ways of thinking.

Those of us who wish to foster the habits of peacemaking have to be patient toward tension in the classroom. Clearly, classrooms that involve the kind of habits that build peace will be messy, conflicted, and at times painful. This is not necessarily a sign that there is a lack of peace but rather likely a sign that the hard work of peacebuilding is taking place. If we know this ahead of time, we can respect the pain of peacebuilding as well as hold on to the promise of peacemaking.

## NOTES

1. bell hooks, *Teaching to Transgress: Education as the Practice of Freedom* (New York: Routledge, 1994), 12.

2. David Johnson and Frank Johnson, *Joining Together: Group Theory and Group Skills,* 5th ed. (Needham Heights, Mass.: Allyn & Bacon, 1994), 306.

3. Stephen D. Brookfield, *Becoming a Critically Reflective Teacher* (San Francisco: Jossey-Bass, 1995), 5.

4. Joan Chodorow, ed., *Jung on Active Imagination* (Princeton, N.J.: Princeton University Press, 1997), 58–59 (emphasis added).

5. Katharina von Kellenbach considers Christian anti-Judaism to be fueled by this kind of "scapegoating." "Scapegoating occurs when human beings cannot bear ambiguity but idealize themselves, their community or beliefs. The purity of a group or doctrine is maintained by projecting unwelcome aspects onto an Other." See *Anti-Judaism in Feminist Religious Writings* (Atlanta: Scholars Press, 1994), 47.

6. Matthew Fox, *Meditations with Meister Eckhart* (Santa Fe, N.Mex.: Bear & Company, 1983), 99.

7. Johnson and Johnson, *Joining Together,* 255.

8. John Stuart Mill, *On Liberty* (Suffolk: Penguin Classics, 1974), 116.

9. See my discussion of this Psalm in Carol Lakey Hess and Marie Hess, "Creativity," in *Way to Live: Christian Practices for Teens,* ed. Dorothy Bass and Don Richter (Nashville: Upper Room, 2002), esp. 105–8.

10. See Walter J. Ong, *Fighting for Life: Contest, Sexuality, and Consciousness* (Amherst: University of Massachusetts Press, 1981); Mary Field Belenky et al.,

*Women's Ways of Knowing: The Development of Self, Voice, and Mind* (New York: Basic Books, 1986).

11. Deborah Tannen, *The Argument Culture: Stopping America's War of Words* (New York: Ballantine Books, 1998).

12. Ibid., 26.

13. Susan Moller Okin, with respondents, *Is Multiculturalism Bad for Women?* ed. Joshua Cohen, Matthew Howard, and Martha C. Nussbaum (Princeton, N.J.: Princeton University Press, 1999).

14. Brookfield, *Becoming a Critically Reflective Teacher,* xvii.

15. Amitai Etzioni, *The New Golden Rule: Community and Morality in a Democratic Society* (New York: Basic Books, 1996), 231.

16. Iris Marion Young, *Justice and the Politics of Difference* (Princeton, N.J.: Princeton University Press, 1990), 236, chapter 8.

17. Brookfield, *Becoming a Critically Reflective Teacher,* 23–25.

18. See Peggy McIntosh, "White Privilege and Male Privilege: A Personal Account of Coming to See Correspondences through Work in Women's Studies," in *Race, Class and Gender: An Anthology,* ed. Margaret L. Andersen and Patricia Hill Collins (Belmont, Calif.: Wadsworth Publishing Co., 1992).

19. Carol Christ, "Toward a Paradigm Shift in the Academy and in Religious Studies," in *The Impact of Feminist Research in the Academy,* ed. Christie Farnham (Indianapolis: Indiana University Press, 1987).

20. Brookfield, *Becoming a Critically Reflective Teacher,* 23.

21. Alasdair MacIntyre, *After Virtue: A Study in Moral Theory* (Notre Dame, Ind.: University of Notre Dame Press, 1984), 222.

22. I first named this in my essay "Echo's Lament: Teaching, Mentoring, and the Dangers of Narcissistic Pedagogy," *Teaching Theology & Religion* 6, no. 3 (July 2003): 127–37.

23. Katheryn Pfisterer Darr, "Ezekiel's Justifications of God: Teaching Troubling Texts," *JSOT* 55 (1992): 110.

24. Nancy J. Duff, "How to Discuss Moral Issues Surrounding Homosexuality When You Know You Are Right," in *Homosexuality and Christian Community,* ed. Choon-Leong Seow (Louisville: Westminster John Knox, 1996).

25. See chapter 2 of Mill's essay, "On Liberty of Thought and Discussion."

26. Etzioni, *The New Golden Rule,* 104.

27. Marjorie Hewitt Suchocki, *Divinity and Diversity: A Christian Affirmation of Religious Pluralism* (Nashville: Abingdon, 2003).

28. Ibid., 84.

29. Young, *Justice and the Politics of Difference,* 236.

30. See Marjorie Hewitt Suchocki, *The Fall to Violence: Original Sin in Relational Theology* (New York: Continuum, 1994). Summarized in *Divinity and Diversity,* 105.

31. Brookfield, *Becoming a Critically Reflective Teacher,* 1.

32. hooks, *Teaching to Transgress,* 42.

# CHAPTER SIX

# Nonviolent Conflicts and Cultural Differences

## Essentials for Practicing Peace

*Kathleen J. Greider*

To the average person, peacebuilding can seem beyond reach. It tends to evoke images of huge distances and proportions: mass demonstrations, international summits, and global concord. It can seem the work of a privileged few people with opportunity and power to contribute directly to the macro-level diplomacy of national and transnational peacebuilding. Even so, all of us daily have opportunities to build peace at the micro-level, in disputes much closer to home — in our families, congregations, workplaces, neighborhoods, and other communities.

The language of peacebuilding can contribute to the seeming inaccessibility of peace, because it tends to evoke images of ubiquitous harmony. We speak of *cease*fires, the *end* of hostilities, peace *agreements*, *United* Nations. The language of managing, mediating, negotiating, arbitrating, resolving, and transforming conflict often sidesteps the reality that we live amid old conflicts that do not yield to our techniques and new conflicts that quickly take the places of the ones that do. Though there has never been a period of peace without conflict, the image of peace as nonconflictual endures. Knowing well our inability to craft in ourselves or our relationships perfect harmony unsullied by conflicts, such language contributes to our sense that peacebuilding is done by special persons who have the magnanimity to model perfect harmony.

None of us, however, needs relinquish the power of peacebuilding to the apparently saintly, because conflict itself has a role in peacebuilding. Until such time that humans are perfect and cease to irritate and harm one another, peace — if we are to have it at all — will have to coexist with conflict. Short of the realm of G-d, the measure of peace cannot be the absence of conflict. Because of human limitation, wrongdoing, and strife, peace is measured not by the absence of conflict, or only by the resolution of conflict, but by honesty about the ongoing reality of conflicts and *nonviolence in the conflicts themselves*. With this standard, all of us can contribute to peacebuilding by engaging necessary conflict with honesty, perseverance, and nonviolence.

In the United States, increasing cultural pluralism is a pressing context in which both our potential contributions to peacebuilding and the realities of ongoing conflict come home to average people. Interactions with persons of other religions, ethnicities, native languages, and nationalities occur with increasing frequency. But these are only the newest forms of cultural plurality. Citizens of the United States have lived for generations amid many other forms of diversity; differences in class, gender, age, region, and education, for example, have long formed distinct cultures that make day-to-day interactions challenging. These interactions are not always conflictual; indeed, sometimes we are drawn together in peaceful harmony by differences that are intriguing and pleasing. At least as often, however, cultural differences are laden with fear and power dynamics that cause conflicts. Thinking that peace requires the absence of conflict, many of us feel that our cultural clashes are wrong and detrimental to peace. Consequently, many of us try to withdraw from one another when conflicts arise in an effort to avoid harmful fighting or even the discomfort of disagreements. Failing that, we are drawn into struggles in which we often harm each other psychospiritually, if not physically.

Intercultural encounters dramatize that neither violent conflict nor avoidance of it can build a meaningful, lasting peace. Rather, as practitioners of nonviolent resistance have demonstrated, meaningful and lasting peace frequently requires us to engage in everyday conflicts, but to do so nonviolently, with a peacebuilding spirit. Average people can contribute to global peace by navigating nonviolently the everyday conflicts caused by cultural differences. But putting these peacebuilding principles into practice requires the development of particular psychospiritual capacities and new behaviors.

Using intercultural encounters as an example and the Christian tradition as a resource, in this essay I explore how nonviolent conflict and cultural differences — especially cultural pluralism in conflict practices — can help construct a meaningful and lasting peace. I describe differences in conflict practices that pertain to the wide range of cultures noted above — the differences in conflict behavior we experience between, for example, female and male, adolescents and their parents, and urban and rural people, as well as those that emerge between people of different ethnic cultures. As a pastoral theologian and caregiver, I am concerned to go beyond ideals to address the grueling psychospiritual and relational demands inherent in our ideal of peace. What capacities of soul does nonviolent conflict require of us? How can we develop such capacities of soul so that we embody with consistency, personally and socially, those peace-promoting behaviors? What can we learn from intercultural encounters about the prevalence of conflict, the importance of nonviolent conflict in peacebuilding, and the characteristics of nonviolent conflict? It is my thesis that respectful engagement of cultural pluralism in conflict practices can help us practice conflict nonviolently, for the sake of peace.

## NO CONFLICT, NO JUSTICE

Peacebuilders cannot reject or avoid conflict, because conflict is an essential part of creating justice among us. Without justice, the appearance of peace is a sham, and not lasting. Indeed, conflicts usually have their genesis in injustices or other forms of unfairness, especially conflicts that have lasted too long and not been resolved by genteel means. When we fight, we are usually fighting *back*. We fight in response to a perceived attack. Wounded and furious, we fight to attempt to protect ourselves from further harm. We fight because not fighting hasn't stopped the unfairness. We fight to bring attention to our ignored suffering and to jumpstart processes that might set things right, at least for future generations. Thus, whether conscious or unconscious, our rejection or avoidance of conflict is often a strategy to avoid consciousness of unfairness and injustice, the history of conflict avoidance that has festered the original injustice, the suffering caused by the history of injustice, and the work of setting things right.

More catastrophically, the rejection or avoidance of conflict is a way of rejecting or avoiding both analyzing power and reforming how it is distributed. Without this analysis and reform there will never be meaningful and lasting peace. Such power dynamics contribute to conflict when power is hoarded by some and denied to others, actually and/or experientially. Often the main reason we avoid power analysis is that it tends to reveal historical, unjust power dynamics that must be changed if we are to build peace. So, for example, we sometimes avoid conflict in contexts where we are disempowered, because the requisite power analysis might reveal that we ought to marshal more power, an always demanding and sometimes dangerous practice. Sometimes our conflict avoidance surfaces in situations where we are empowered, because power analysis might reveal that we ought to relinquish some of our power, and too few of us have the spiritual constitution to embrace this peacebuilding practice.

For the sake of reform and justice, peacebuilders must not reject or avoid conflict. There is no lasting peace without justice, and there is no justice without conflict. Indeed, from this perspective, we can say that where such important values are at stake, peacebuilders ought to work not only for less violence but also for more conflicts. The "peace-with-justice" so widely promoted in peacebuilding cannot be attained without spending time in the wilderness of not-yet-resolved conflict, where wrongs are recounted, fury given vent, the ruins of relationship and other damages acknowledged, remorse and reparation cultivated, and anguish expressed and heard.

## PRACTICING CONFLICT — NONVIOLENTLY — IS PRACTICING PEACE

Of course, lasting peace is not built by means of violent conflict. The kind of conflict participation I am advocating excludes threats and acts of physical violence, psychospiritual violence (such as cruelty and shaming), and social violence (such as discrimination and impoverishment). Some people assume that violence is inevitably a part of conflict, but this assumption is inaccurate. Though violence obviously is sometimes a part of conflict, conflict is not defined by negativity or violation. Rather, as noted in the previous section, conflict is essential to positive ends, such as resistance to wrongdoing and the creation of just relations.

The honorable and honored tradition of nonviolence has nonviolent conflict at its heart. The philosophy and practice of nonviolent resistance does not support the avoidance of conflict but provides ways, without causing harm, of participating in a conflict in order to fight for justice. Nonviolence is attractive to many because of its peacefulness. By itself, however, the peacefulness of nonviolence does not make it effective. Nonviolence is effective because it is a movement toward conflict, before resolution is assured. Nonviolence is effective because it engages disputants respectfully, insisting on the cessation of violence, but not the cessation of conflict. Nonviolence is effective because, through the cessation of violence, it helps craft a dignified and honorable conflict, in which nuances of the dispute and the possibility of resolution can be explored.

Conflict resolution strategies warn against moving too quickly to res-olution, trying to bypass the fight itself. But most of us do just that—try to move too quickly to resolution. That is, if we are able to subdue our impulse to return hurt for hurt, the next impulse is usually to get this fight over with as soon as possible. Management of a conflict, much less peacebuilding, cannot begin, however, until all participants can be present to the dispute, nonviolently, as long as necessary for peaceful-ness to be built collaboratively. In the heat of a conflict, there is much work to be done before we get to the processes by which a conflict might be resolved. Wrongdoing must be identified without minimiz-ing or exaggerating, thoughts and feelings expressed and listened to by all parties, responsibility determined, and remorse felt and demon-strated. Moreover, we will undoubtedly persist in causing one another grievances. Therefore, a lasting peace occurs not because conflict is abolished, or not only because a specific conflict is resolved, but also because the people(s) involved learn to engage the heat of the argu-ment nonviolently the next time an injustice occurs between them, as it surely will. Thus, it is not just that those who would practice peace must learn to get through conflict or to manage, mediate, negotiate, arbitrate, resolve, and transform conflict, though these too are essen-tial for peace and peacebuilding. We must also develop the spiritual capacity to be *in* conflict, to stay in the thick of it for a while — not just get through it — and to do so nonviolently.

It is possible to be in conflict with someone without harming her/him, to speak difficult truths in a spirit of love (Eph. 4:15). The final section of the essay explores specific cultural differences in conflict that, when held in tension, help us maintain nonviolence in conflict. In the following section, however, I address three general aspects of nonviolent conflict practice that are foundational to those specifics and provide partial standards by which violent and nonviolent conflict can be differentiated. Nonviolent conflict practices serve life, facilitate honest dialogue, and require power analyses from start to finish.

### Nonviolent Conflict Practices Serve Life

Christian tradition tells us that Jesus of Nazareth lived so that others could have life, and have it abundantly (John 10:10). In this spirit, Christians engage nonviolently in conflict only for the purpose of increasing abundance of life for all. While violent conflict is death-dealing, conflict is kept nonviolent by assuring that it is life-enhancing, that it serves the common good. Indeed, we are called to engage in nonviolent conflict when it is essential for the construction of new, more abundant life. The fair distribution of power that enables abundance of life rarely happens voluntarily or without a struggle. Therefore, we use nonviolent conflict to assure that all — in this generation and the ones to come — enjoy life abundant. The definition of conflict offered by congregational consultant Caroline Westerhoff articulates this positive force: conflict is the birth of something new.[1] The birth of something new is rarely if ever accomplished without difficulty and strife; consider, for example, the birthing of children, the birthing of sobriety, and the birthing of new social orders. Nonetheless, the pain of birthing new life is very often a pain worth bearing.

### Nonviolent Conflict Practices Facilitate Honest Dialogue

Nonviolent conflict does not accomplish its purposes without dialogue that is full of the integrity that often manifests in discomfort. We violate one another if in conflict we shy away from pain, shirk responsibility, practice dishonesty, or in some other way fail to take up the work of doing right by one another. For conflict to be nonviolent, we must strive for dialogue that has integrity: genuineness, truth, reliability. Such honest and deep dialogue is, very often, excruciating. When practical theologian Carol Lakey Hess writes about "hard dialogue," her words also describe nonviolent conflict.

> Hard dialogue presumes and fosters genuine relationality; it is dialogue that allows participants to ask difficult and ofttimes painful questions. Deep and authentic connections can result only when

we have argued, dialogued, and conversed in such a manner with one another.[2]

In nonviolent conflict we strive not to harm one another. Still, the conflict itself will likely be painful. In honest and deep communication, we discover not only our confirming similarities and happy agreements but also our destabilizing differences and divisive disagreements. In nonviolent conflict we engage in hard dialogue not for the purpose of hurting one another but, as noted above, for the purpose of forging something new between us, for the sake of life abundant and the common good.

## Nonviolent Conflict Practices Require Power Analysis

Integrity in nonviolent conflict communication raises many hard issues, but no dialogue is harder — or, more encouragingly, more full of integrity and the promise of peace — than power analysis. For our purposes, power analysis refers to the process by which we examine every conflict to illuminate the actual and perceived power[3] at play in the conflict, identify persons and groups that have excess and insufficient power, and create more just power distribution through nonviolent conflict and its resolution. Power analysis is more complicated than claiming that some participants in a conflict are powerful while others are powerless. Power analysis seeks to engage the dynamic interaction, particular to each conflict and the people involved, of many complex factors, including:

- cultural differences in the interpretation of power
- sociohistorical experiences of power among the peoples involved
- the impact of perceptions of power as well as the distribution of actual power
- the relativity of power: for example, white women tend to have insufficient power in gender conflicts and excess power in racial-ethnic conflicts

For Christians, Episcopal priest and conflict consultant Eric Law helpfully suggests that in power analysis of a given conflict we are determining where we are in what he calls the cycle of gospel living.[4] He notes that the Christian life is a recurring movement between the powerlessness of the cross and the powerfulness of resurrection. Christians are sometimes called to be people of the cross, sacrificing and emptying ourselves, and we are sometimes called to be people of the resurrection, empowering and filling ourselves, both for the sake of love. Power analysis involves determining whether, in a particular conflict situation, love requires us to enter the cycle of gospel living at the place of the cross, where we relinquish power, or at the place of resurrection, where we embrace power. Over time, if we are not abusing either the cross or the resurrection, we move back and forth between these approaches to gospel living. Over time, this kind of gospel living increases our intellectual and spiritual capabilities to discern whether, in a given situation, our contribution to peace in that conflict is cross or resurrection, and to embrace either path nonviolently.

Nonviolent conflict practices take practice. They do not come naturally, but they can be learned. Like practicing a musical instrument or a sport, much learning happens through repetition and trial and error. Because of their increasing frequency, and because cultural plurality can be provocative of violence, intercultural encounters are important arenas for the practice of nonviolent conflict.

## CULTURAL DIVERSITY AND CONFLICT CUSTOMS: PRACTICING NONVIOLENT CONFLICT

Ironically, in intercultural encounters we often are in conflict over our ways of being in conflict. It can be argued that "peace" and "conflict" have some meanings that can be generalized across cultures of religion, ethnicity, gender, class, etc. However, because our experiences of conflict are always located in specific times, places, value systems, and relationships, culturally specific meanings and relational patterns tend to obscure shared meanings. In cultures' many dimensions, we are taught ways of handling conflict that are deemed appropriate within those cultures but are often in stark contrast with other cultures' approaches to conflict. The culture of gender, for example, tends to teach divergent conflict lessons to little girls ("be nice") and to little boys ("be strong"). When we encounter these differing culture-specific conflict customs in conflicts, we tend to treat them as oppositional and competing and to experience the difference as additional violation. The original dispute is exacerbated by a dispute over proper conduct in disputes.

The demands of navigating conflicts with a peacebuilding spirit are exemplified amid the psychospiritual challenges of conflictual cultural differences. It is not merely coincidental that the biblical image of the Peaceable Realm — so often invoked as the epitome of nonviolence — portrays a future peace between currently warring species.

> The wolf shall dwell with the lamb, and the leopard shall lie
> down with the kid,
> and the calf and the lion and the fatling together,
> and a little child shall lead them.
> The cow and the bear shall feed; their young lie down together;
> and the lion shall eat straw like the ox.
> The sucking child shall play over the hole of the asp,
> and the weaned child shall put his hand on the adder's den.
> They shall not hurt or destroy in all my holy mountain;
> for the earth shall be full of the knowledge of YHWH as the
> waters cover the sea. (Isa. 11:6–9)

This passage is beloved for the hope it offers in the face of what seem intractable, even life-threatening conflicts. At its heart is a sobering challenge. Eric Law puts the challenge into plain talk:

> In order for the animals to co-exist in this Peaceable Realm, very "unnatural" behaviors are required from all involved. How can a

wolf, a leopard, or a lion not attack a lamb, a calf, or a child for food? . . . How can a lamb or a calf not run when it sees a lion or a leopard coming close? How can a lion eat straw like an ox when a lion is known to be a meat eater? It goes against an animal's "instinct" to be in this vision of the Peaceable Realm. Perhaps that is what is required of human beings if we are to live together peacefully with each other.[5]

The remainder of the essay is dedicated to envisioning practices that embrace the challenge at the heart of this beloved image. I offer descriptions of some conflict behaviors that, because of socialization within our cultures, seem to come "naturally."[6] Unfortunately, the conflict behaviors that come naturally to our culture(s) often feel like violations to persons of other cultures. If we are serious about building a nonviolent, peaceable realm, we need to moderate these behaviors. But how is it possible to moderate behavior that feels so natural? What "unnatural" behaviors are required of us?

The Peaceable Realm is portrayed as a place where all the animals stop insisting on their own way. They learn from each other and moderate their own behavior by following the good example of their opposites. The carnivorous lion starts eating straw, like the ox. The wolves and the leopards become gentler, like the lambs and the kids. The lambs and the kids become bolder, like the wolves and the leopards. In this way, our societies are not merely multicultural but become intercultural, as we not merely tolerate but engage and seek to learn from our differences. Following the image of the Peaceable Realm, I use cultural diversity to identify seven spectrums of human experience on which apparent opposites in our natural conflict behaviors emerge. I discuss how these opposites in conflict behavior do not have to be oppositional but can be complementary to one another. I try to show that cultural differences are not necessarily mutually exclusive but can be "mutually corrective."[7]

This mutual help is possible because at the heart of these cultural opposites are common human needs and quests: we try by very different means to find answers to persistent human questions. Cultural differences in conflict approaches can help us see options for feeling, behavior, and relationship that we otherwise could not have imagined. Moderating our most natural behaviors by learning from that which is opposite and thoughtfully trying out unnatural behavior help us move beyond mere multiculturality to interculturality, but also may help us reach our deep desires, such as nonviolent conflict and peace. One example: some Christians' capacity for peacefulness is increased by sustained practice of Buddhist meditation.

Flexibility in conflict practices is not the norm and will likely feel unnatural, at least at first. Normally, our cultural particularities cause us to become entrenched toward one or the other end of these spectrums. But neither does the nonviolent, peacebuilding spirit allow for rigid adherence to any one location on these spectrums. Peacebuilding amid cultural plurality requires us to keep our focus on the common human needs at issue on each spectrum; it requires us to learn from each other a dynamic interculturality in our conflict behaviors, and to develop enough flexibility in conflict styles to move along these spectrums as appropriate to the situation.

## TOWARD THE PEACEABLE REALM: INTERCULTURALITY IN CONFLICT CUSTOMS

At least seven common human quests and spectrums of practices are at play in intercultural conflicts.

- How do we survive? The spectrum of self and others

- Where do we belong? The spectrum of "us" and "them"

- How do we manage uncertainty? The spectrum of knowing and not-knowing

- How do we communicate? The spectrum of directness and indirectness

- How do we express our agency and power? The spectrum of restraint and initiative

- How do we express our deep convictions? The spectrum of fervency and discretion

- How do we adjudicate our differences? The spectrum of mainte-nance and change

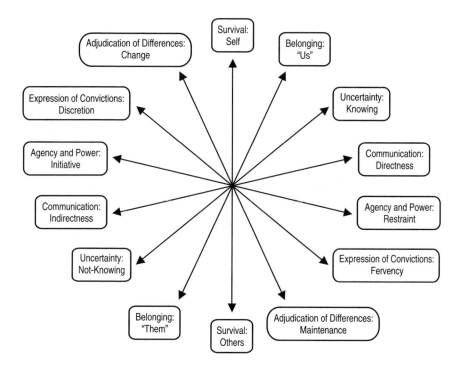

Peacebuilding lies at the intersection of these common human quests and differences in conflict practices.

The cultural differences identified in the following discussion are tendencies, not pure types. Within all cultures, some people's behavior varies from — even rebels against — cultural norms and socialization. To avoid violating each other by using these tendencies as stereotypes, we must always be alert and responsive to exceptions.

## *How Do We Survive? The Spectrum of Self and Others*

Cultural differences in conflict reveal a spectrum of values, attitudes, and behaviors ranging from individualism to altruism. This spectrum of behaviors arises in large measure out of our instinct to survive and its related fight/flight impulse. While conflict avoidance expresses the impulse to protect survival by fleeing, our behaviors *in* conflict express the impulse to protect survival by fighting anything that feels life-threatening — threatening to body or soul, to us or to others. If peace is to be built, it is crucial in a conflict to bear in mind, with empathy, that something has happened to cause us and/or our opponents to feel that life is threatened. Our opponents, like us, feel they are fighting for life itself. To those enamored with human evolution and rationality, this may seem overly dramatic. However, just and lasting peace requires that we diminish our naïveté about — and respond with more empathy toward — the primal, finely honed, barely conscious sensitivity humans have regarding threats to life and the frequency with which humans are fighting threats to soul as well as to physical life.

Where life is threatened, some cultural contexts most highly value self-support: in these cultures, I am thought to be mature when I am able to take care of my own needs through self-reliance. Other cultures, when threatened, most highly value supporting others: in these cultures, I am thought to be mature when I am able to take care of the needs of others through self-denial. The cultures of gender stereotypically exemplify these different approaches to survival. Boys and men tend to be taught individualism — to take care of themselves through self-reliance. Girls and women tend to be taught altruism — to take care of others through self-sacrifice. Advocacy for one's own survival and altruistic assurance of the survival of others are often posed as competitive, even irreconcilable conflict strategies, but both are essential to nonviolence and peace.

No other initial conflict-response strategy is more effective than altruism. The ability to put our own agenda aside temporarily and seek first to understand the concerns of our dispute partners expresses re-spect for the sanctity of life, including that of our opponents. But because all life is sacred, including the life in us, at some point in-dividualism is required in order to express respect for the sanctity of life in the self, such as in situations of self-defense. If we say that all life is sacred but only deny the self, then the truth is not in us.

Altruism is an effective first response in conflict also because it is an emergency response to our dispute partners' sense that spiritual or phys-ical survival is at risk. Altruism enables us to join forces with our dispute partner to reduce the threat to life. In good time, of course, we must give ourselves a similar emergency response. Without individualism, we never practice any self-defense. If we deny too long the threats to self, we die, literally or metaphorically, and are no use to others or to G-d. Or, sensing the threat of death, our impulse to survive can engender a flood of individualism that drowns our altruism. We encounter this phenomenon when formerly altruistic people — now literally selfless — flee their responsibilities to go in search of themselves.

If conflict is to be fully nonviolent and peace just and lasting, we need to learn from each other to practice a flexible combination of al-truism and individualism. Both are needed to resist violence: altruism resists violence against others, individualism resists violence against the self. Both are needed to assure that all persons are fully alive and able to contribute to the hard work of peacebuilding. Practicing a flex-ible combination of both altruism and individualism is a peacebuilding reminder that self and other are interconnected, not fully distinct. Threats to others are threats to self, and vice versa. No one survives alone. Altruism cares for the self, individualism cares for others.

### Where Do We Belong?
### The Spectrum of "Us" and "Them"

Martin Buber's notion of the I-Thou relationship[8] captures the imagi-nation of so many because it voices our yearning for holy relatedness but also because, by implication, it admits to the gap between us. The boundaries of our physical-psychic selves are somewhat permeable, but they also cause concrete and spiritual distance between self and others. In many conflict situations, we and our opponents are fighting against the anxiety of aloneness. The result is a spectrum of values, attitudes, and behaviors ranging from what I call "Us" to "Them," on which a primary value is the sense of belonging.[9] Sometimes we are fighting for "us": groups where we feel we belong, people like us, who share our values and characteristics. Sometimes we are fighting for "them": groups to which we might like to belong, people not like us but appealingly different, whose values and characteristics we appreciate and advocate. Teenagers, with their passion to belong and their passion for justice, are among the few groups able to fight passionately on behalf of both "us" and "them."

It is difficult to overstate the power that the quest for belonging exerts on us. We explored in the previous section that threats to our survival sometimes drive us to fight, but it is also true that for many of us, there is no point to surviving if we do not feel that we belong somewhere, that we matter to someone. Suicide has many causes, and one is the feeling that we do not belong and are alone. Membership in violent gangs illustrates the converse: members put themselves at great risk of death because in the gang they belong, they know the feeling of family.

It is nearly impossible to identify any culture that does not value behavior loyal to "us." There are, however, some cultures that value it almost exclusively; many of my African and Pacific Islander students, for example, say that their cultures are "we-cultures," where they are judged to have matured when they are fully rooted in and dedicated to the welfare of the families or villages to which they belong. Alternatively, while very few cultures do not value behavior loyal to "us," there are some cultures that place significant value on seeking out "them." In these cultures, I am believed to have matured when I am engaged with my primary group — my family, mainly — but also have a spirit of risk, adventure, and advocacy that takes me beyond "us" to "them" — groups different from my primary groups.

In the work of peacebuilding, there is arguably no more important or difficult task than breaking down the dividing walls between "us" and "them." Because "us"/"them" dynamics have contributed so significantly to violence, a peacebuilder's impulse may understandably be to minimize such distinctions. But because belonging is a cornerstone of human health and well-being, it is both futile and counterproductive to resist this force of nature. Instead, we need to work toward a combination of healthy "us" and "them" behaviors. On the one hand, we can work for peace by increasing havens in which people have the experience that they fit in, feel at home, are recognizable to others, and can let down their guard. Amid conflict, we need "us" experiences because they enable us to relax, rest, and rebuild our energies for entering again into the demands of engaging difference. Monocultural groups are often criticized by those excluded from them, but they serve this essential function and help build the peace.

On the other hand, we can work for peace by increasing the opportunities for adventuresome encounter between "us" and "them." The power of this dynamic is illustrated in the organization Seeds of Peace,[10] which in its first year brought together a group of Israeli, Palestinian, and Egyptian youth designated by their governments as "future leaders." Seeing in each other the human face of the "them" they were taught to hate was powerful enough to reduce the fear that breeds violence. But, more positively, such travel and encounter makes possible experiences in which being with "those people" decreases aloneness and yields a sense of belonging. Stunningly, this sense of belonging to "them" promises a brighter future for "us." Such encounters strengthen our sense of belonging to both "us" and "them."

### How Do We Manage Uncertainty?
### The Spectrum of Knowing and Not-Knowing

Given the enormous ambiguity that characterizes life, and given that uncertainty is a very uncomfortable experience for many people, it is not surprising that cultural plurality reveals a range of values, attitudes, and behaviors dealing with this problem. Sometimes we fight over clear rights and wrongs, but it is not uncommon to be fighting because so much is unclear, indefinite, bewildering. "Managing uncertainty" is one way to articulate the common human task at issue on this spectrum, but we could as accurately call it the quest for wisdom. In a conflict we are often fighting over different cultural formulations of wisdom.

Some cultures place a very high value on knowing. Confidence in the human capacity for comprehension is high and, consequently, a productive "doing" mentality prevails. In these cultures, I am considered mature when, in the face of uncertainty, I have expertise and offer solutions. Where certainty is scarce, I am considered mature if I resist uncertainty with ingenuity, a can-do attitude, experimentation, or even an educated guess. When uncertainty emerges in a conflict, if I am knowledgeable, I am expected to actively provide answers and give direction. If I do not have knowledge, I am expected to deferentially follow the instruction of those whose knowledge is greater than mine. Academic cultures, and other cultures highly influenced by Enlightenment values — many European and European American cultures, for example — consistently demonstrate in conflicts this approach to uncertainty.

Other cultures place a very high value on not-knowing. These cultures place their confidence in the wisdom of the overall environment, of which human knowledge is but a part. Consequently, a state of reflective "being" that seeks to receive wisdom from beyond the human is valued as much as or more than "doing," which is more focused on creating or discovering wisdom from within the human. In these cultures, I am considered mature when I am able to recognize both limits and strengths in my knowledge, suspend my judgments and choices as a part of seeking wisdom that resides beyond me, and strive to practice patient presence and receptivity to all elements of my world. When in a conflict uncertainty is at issue, I am expected to listen in depth and at length to others, immerse myself expectantly in the comprehensions of others, especially if they are contrary to mine, and distill insights until a positive means of proceeding amid uncertainty is glimpsed. The culture of contemplative religious community exemplifies the valuation of not-knowing.

Knowing and not-knowing may seem competitive or irreconcilable strategies, but both are essential to long-lasting peace. On the one hand, if peace is to be built, we cannot be satisfied with a violating stance of disrespect and not-caring that allows ignorance to go unchallenged. Efforts to learn about and from each other go a long way toward peace, because they convey respect and care and lay the cornerstone of the human relatedness without which we have no peace. On the other hand, our heartfelt striving to know must be grounded in a humble assertion of our incapacity to know fully. The metaphor may be reassuring, but we cannot and do not walk in another's shoes and must not violate each other with pseudo-familiarity. Even as we promise to try to understand we must, in the same breath, promise never to assume, never to think too much of our thinking.

David Augsburger's distinction between empathy and what he calls "interpathy" helps us here.[11] While empathy is compassionate understanding built from a starting place of similarity, interpathy is compassionate understanding built from a starting place of not-knowing. In conflict that is nonviolent, we usually are starting from the position of interpathy in regard to the position of our dispute partner(s). There are dimensions of experience where our differences are so significant that the honest and most compassionate thing to say is, "I know I do not understand." Not-knowing is not a stopping place in interpathy, however. We actively seek to educate ourselves about our differences. As a part of our learning, we regard our dispute partners as teachers, people to whom we respectfully offer ourselves as students. In this way, the not-knowing of interpathy seeks to set in motion the teaching and learning that slowly, if we persevere, builds some empathic knowing. The goal in caregiving is not that we eliminate interpathy with empathy — we will never fully know the other.

The most respectful and compassionate caregiving combines a dynamic interplay of both interpathy and empathy.

In the uncertainty of conflict, so much is at stake, such as survival and belonging. Without the ability to embrace not-knowing, we reach for wisdom but settle for answers, however partial or made-up and mistaken. We need not-knowing to temper our panic. Conversely, because there is so much uncertainty, we are also at risk of giving up on wisdom, failing to reach for understanding. We need the ability to seek knowledge that can temper our despair. If we break the bond between knowing and not-knowing, we have arrogance and ignorance, both of which contribute significantly to violence and undermine peace. Our peacebuilding is best served by intercultural learning that cultivates a flexible combination of knowing and not-knowing stances.

## How Do We Communicate?
### The Spectrum of Directness and Indirectness

Arguably no other issue challenges us more in conflict situations than how most effectively to communicate our experience of the situation. Very often we are fighting over whether or not we feel we have been listened to, heard, and understood. Some cultural groups place extraordinary value on unmediated, person-to-person communication. In these cultures, I am considered mature when I address others face-to-face, look my conversation partners in the eye, speak with certainty and precision, and get to the heart of the matter without delay. In a conflict I am expected to approach my dispute partner(s) promptly, before speaking to others, and state my complaint plainly. Other cultural groups place extraordinary value on indirect, mediated communication. In these groups, I am considered mature when I address others with delicacy, through use of allusions and symbols. In a conflict I am expected to take the time to consult with and rely on a wise third party, who then helps me communicate and resolve my grievance.

Differences between educational cultures illustrate some of these differences in communication styles. For example, in the culture of the U.S. educational system, I was taught classroom behaviors such as eye contact and quick, vigorous, and mutual verbal exchange with the teacher and classmates, as well as debates formed of plain talk and clearly argued disagreements. However, most of my students who have been educated in Korea have been taught classroom behavior focused on listening, waiting until invited to speak, and avoiding obvious disagreements, especially with the teacher. These differences not only impede communication but also can cultivate conflicts when, for example, sensitive discussion topics are raised but cannot be fairly explored because students (and teachers) trained in directness tend to overpower students trained in indirectness.

Directness and indirectness in communication are often seen to be oppositional and mutually exclusive, but nonviolent communication teaches us that peace comprises a mixture of both. For example, one of the most incendiary dynamics in conflict is shame, and ability in both directness and indirectness is needed if shame is to be minimized. In cultures that favor direct communication, indirect communication can be experienced as a violation of privacy and betrayal that causes shame and thus aggravates the conflict. In such situations, the values of direct communication — its confidentiality, intimacy, bravery, and hopefulness — shine through. Some of our most touching peace negotiations include some level of direct communication between dispute partners.

However, it is grueling to remain nonviolent during direct, conflictual communication. Cultures that favor direct communication regularly underestimate the skill needed and are not able to live up to their ideal. Faced with an opponent, the difficulties of speaking the truth and doing so with love multiply exponentially. Direct communication between disputants is infamous for devolving into violence or otherwise negative behavior that worsens the conflict. We speak injudiciously, inflict or suffer blame and shame, threaten or harm further, and in other ways aggravate the conflict.

For these reasons, many cultures see direct confrontation as argumentative and humiliating. Cultures that favor indirect communication do so in part because face-to-face communication between opponents often aggravates the conflict: the shame of direct confrontation of conflict is said to cause "loss of face." Mediated, indirect communication is essential when direct communication is dysfunctional or dangerous, as it usually is. Wisely, more and more cultures (including corporate cultures) are calling for the use of skilled coaches and trained mediators who provide the coaching and supervision most of us need if we are to have the maturity, when face-to-face with an opponent, to speak the truth and do so not violently but lovingly. Consultation gives us time and relational space, in anticipation of facing our opponent, to prepare ourselves psychospiritually for nonviolent negotiation and to practice constructive words and behaviors.

Peacebuilding depends on our ability to pursue communication by whatever nonviolent means are necessary. Interculturality teaches us a variety of communication styles — flexible, situation-appropriate combinations of direct and indirect communication. Intercultural clashes teach us that our willingness not to insist on the communication style most comfortable to us but to try on something "unnatural" goes an immeasurable distance toward the nonviolence that makes peace possible.

### How Do We Express Our Agency and Power?
### The Spectrum of Restraint and Initiative

Cultural differences in conflict draw our attention to a range of attitudes and behaviors from restraint to initiative. On this spectrum, we are wrestling with how best to express the internal vitality that is part of our aliveness. The impulse in us to survive and thrive is powerful, and our inborn energies need expression if we are to have a sense of agency, influence, and usefulness. We need both actual power and a perception of that power. Humans thrive, in part, when the exercise of actual power imbues us experientially with the perception that we have made a difference, which, in turn, increases our sense of meaning and worth. If thwarted to excess, we respond with violence, using whatever social, interpersonal, and internal power we have to strike back. Thus, not infrequently, we are fighting to develop or get recognition of these powers or because more constructive use of our energy has been denied us.[12] In some cultural settings, it is persons who express their agency and powers in a reserved and careful style who are thought to be most adept at conflict situations. In other cultural contexts, persons who interact in an openly vigorous fashion are most admired for their way of approaching conflict. Though these approaches are normally seen as mutually exclusive, it is indisputable that both are crucial in peacebuilding practices.

Many conflicts are aggravated by knee-jerk reactions. Restraint keeps us from acting too quickly, without sufficient reflection. Peacebuilding requires that participants "allow gracious time,"[13] and graciousness is composed in part by the slower tempo and patience of restraint. Without restraint, we pile issue on issue on issue; we try to do too much and accomplish less because of it. Restraint is part and parcel of the spiritual disciplines of solitude and meditation, both of which are critical elements in the demandingly thoughtful participation required for conflict mediation. Restraint of ourselves offers a safer space to others for the expression of their deepest convictions, and without the airing of these, no peace can last. If we do not restrain ourselves, we do not listen, and without listening, there will be not even a truce, much less peace. Restraint makes possible the delicate touch often required in the care of conflicts: some conflicts need acupuncture, not surgery.[14]

But just as it is possible to move too fast in a conflict, it is also possible to move too slowly. Conflicts are frequently aggravated by avoidance and procrastination. The biblical metaphor of not letting the sun go down on our anger is not intended to encourage haste but rather to discourage us from stewing during long sleepless nights. Sometimes peacebuilding processes are stymied by the carefulness of restraint, and initiative makes possible a risky or unexpected thing that brings fresh air and fresh energy into the deliberations. Without initiative, we do not speak, and no one sets the peacebuilding process in motion; hurts pile up, making the work of peacebuilding harder than if we had responded more promptly. Initiative has value in conflict when it energizes us to care promptly for a wound and thus decrease the chances that it will fester, swell, and spread. One of the most powerful values of initiative is affirmed in guidance attributed to Jesus:

> If you are offering your gift at the altar, and there remember that your brother has something against you, leave your gift there before the altar and go; first be reconciled to your brother, and then come and offer your gift. (Matt. 5:23–24)

Sometimes peaceful, Christ-like living is cultivated by taking initiative to seek out the wounded, especially those who feel wounded by us.

We need a flexible combination of restraint and initiative to keep conflict nonviolent and thereby to build peace. Interculturality teaches us how our ways of exercising agency and power affect our dispute partners: initiative can overpower restraint, restraint can capitulate to initiative. Nonviolence requires that we modulate the expression of our most core energies for the sake of the other. If we are inclined to restraint, we can help build the peace by examining initiative for its good value and receiving or practicing initiative where it serves the common good. If we are inclined toward initiative, we can help build the peace by meeting more restrained others on their terms — perhaps through the indirectness discussed above — and listen at length, speak delicately, or take time out for solitude and reflection.

### How Do We Express Our Deep Convictions? The Spectrum of Fervency and Discretion

In some cultural contexts, the most mature and constructive position to take in a conflict is to work to keep things cool, while in others, the heat of the argument is a positive measure of honesty and a more authentic resolution. I have a friend of Italian heritage who says that her family's pointed and vociferous interactions were not fights, as they appeared to many of her non-Italian friends, but merely fervent discussions of important issues. In contrast, Emma and Martyn Percy write about the "passionate coolness" expected of discussants in their British Anglican context, which emphasizes discretion, politeness, and patience.[15] The differences in these approaches to conflict may obscure that a common human task is at their core: how best to expose our most passionate thoughts and feelings. Our fights are usually grounded in deep convictions but also in differences over the most appropriate manner to speak of the most important things. Value judgments run rampant between cultures around these differences and preoccupy us from the necessity in peacebuilding for both abilities.

If peace is to be made, we must cultivate the capacity to "sit in the fire."[16] This may seem easy for those of us with hot tempers, but we need to sit in the fires not only of our inner passions and hurts but in those of others. The heat in a person and an argument is a clue — one often difficult to read, admittedly — that we are drawing closer to the things that matters most. We may well fight to the death over the things that matter most to us, so we flee or quash the heat to the peril of all. Sometimes our own inner heat signals values that we hold inside but hold fiercely nonetheless. Sometimes the heat is obvious to all — a fierce person or group arguing values in public. In either case, the points where conflicts get most fiery are invaluable guideposts toward the deepest layers of the conflict, which may be previously unconscious in us or others. Moreover, the heat of an argument may also be a cautionary signal that we are approaching a wound in us or others. It is often in the area of our deepest convictions that we are most vulnerable and, frequently, in those soft spots we also carry wounds. As we know from the healing of our bodies, wounds often get warm or hot before they start to heal. Without the capacity to be near the heat of a conflict, we are unequipped to be present to the deepest passions and wounds of others and our relationships. A hot wound ignored sometimes heals on its own, but just as often it degenerates into infection. Of course, some wounds need to be iced as part of their healing, and here we turn to the value of coolness in conflict.

Precisely because heat is a given in conflict, we need times of cooling. Cooling a conflict does not rest on extinguishing all fire — which is not possible, needed, or peace-promoting — but to increase the level of safety so that the fire can be fought with less loss of life. The contribution of coolness to peacebuilding is greatest when it serves to contain a conflict on the verge of becoming violent, for example, by introducing more restraint or indirectness. A cool head can also bring added perspective; when the miracle of shared laughter happens in a conflict, it is usually because someone with a cool head was able to see and gently convey some humor peeking through the seriousness.

It is a combination of heat and coolness that best advances our peacebuilding in intercultural conflicts. Both cool tempers and hot tempers can be used to aggravate others and so, in this spectrum, for the sake of peace, all of us are called not to fan conflict's flames with provocation either by excess or withholding. We must strive to be like firefighters: approach heat, but always with a cool head. We must feel the fire and be able to think about it at the same time, able to access rationality and bravery in the same movement. We must teach ourselves to know when and where it is best not to fight a fire but to let it burn itself out. As a parent has noted, when the kids are cranky from exhaustion after a long day, it is usually better to try to remain cool than to respond in kind, because after a night's sleep, the conflict will usually have died out. In some situations, however, if we are too invested in the mere appearance of peace, we may miss smoldering hot spots that later explode into inferno.

### How Do We Adjudicate Our Differences?
### The Spectrum of Maintenance and Change

In a conflict, most participants are struggling with how to bring it to an end. At issue on this spectrum of behaviors are differences in power between the disputing parties, especially social power, and how those power differentials come into play as we try to resolve our disputes. Almost always, we are fighting over how we use or try to gain power in order to settle a dispute. In situations where a cultural group has actual and/or perceived power, participation in conflict is shaped to a significant degree toward maintaining or increasing that power. As a member of a group with perceived or actual power, I am considered mature when I act to preserve that power through upholding the patterns that create it. In contrast, in a situation where a cultural group lacks actual or perceived power, participation in a conflict is shaped to a significant degree toward systemic change that will increase its power. As a member of a group with insufficient perceived or actual power, I am considered mature when I act to change the patterns that distribute power and thus increase the actual and perceived power of my culture.

Maintenance and change seem to be not only opposite but conflicting strategies. However, employing power analysis in cultural clashes helps us see that we need to have the capacity for both maintaining and changing power arrangements and, especially, the wisdom to know when each is needed. Parents and teachers, for example, must not simply abdicate all their power when in conflict with children. Rather, the moral and caring thing to do is to maintain sufficient power to protect and guide children and to change the power dynamics as children are more able to navigate the world without adult influence. Similarly, when the different cultures of political parties lead to conflict, we do not want our elected officials to simply relinquish power for the sake of conflict resolution. We want them to maintain enough power to work for the common good and change as necessary to strike meaningful compromises. Power dynamics contribute to conflict when power is hoarded by some and denied to others, actually and/or experientially. When we find ourselves in an interpersonal conflict because of ethnic cultural differences, a complete surrender of our power does not help to set things right. Paradoxically, a lasting peace in ethnic-racial conflict usually requires that we maintain enough power to participate in changing the systems that distribute power.

Interculturality teaches us that both strategies of maintenance — conservation of power, invocation of tradition, protection of rights and responsibilities — and strategies of change — redistribution of power, challenge of tradition, and rearrangement of rights and responsibilities — have value. Power analysis helps us discern the degree to which the nonviolent and just resolution of a conflict requires some maintenance of the current power arrangements and/or some change in the distribution of power.

## NONVIOLENT CONFLICT REPRISED

There is no peace without justice, and no justice without conflict. Everyday people contribute to the building of peace, not by avoiding conflict but by striving to be nonviolent in our conflicts and use them to increase justice. Cultural diversity in conflict practices reveals that there are many more ways of being in conflict than we had thought possible. Though at first it feels unnatural to stray from our usual ways of being in conflict, greater interculturality in conflict practices increases the likelihood of nonviolence and our realization of the Peaceable Realm.

## NOTES

1. Caroline A. Westerhoff, "The Birthing of the New," in *Conflict Management in Congregations,* ed. David B. Lott (Bethesda, Md.: Alban Institute, 2001), 54–61.

2. Carol Lakey Hess, "Education as an Art of Getting Dirty with Dignity," in *The Arts of Ministry: Feminist-Womanist Approaches,* ed. Christie Cozad Neuger (Louisville: Westminster John Knox, 1996), 65.

3. The many kinds of power at play in a conflict include sociopolitical, economic, religious, spiritual, physical, and interpersonal powers, to name only a few.

4. Eric H. F. Law, *The Wolf Shall Dwell with the Lamb: A Spirituality for Leadership in a Multicultural Community* (St. Louis: Chalice Press, 1993), 74.

5. Ibid., 3–4.

6. For other differences at play in intercultural encounters and additional strategies for response, see David Augsburger, *Conflict Mediation across Cultures: Pathways and Patterns* (Louisville: Westminster/John Knox, 1992).

7. Fulgence Nyengele, "Consciousness of Context in Pastoral Care and the Issue of Multiculturalism," *Journal of Theology* 104 (Summer 2000): 37.

8. Martin Buber, *I and Thou*, trans. Ronald Gregor Smith (Edinburgh: T. & T. Clark, 1937). The "I-Thou" relationship is one in which we treat the other not as an "it," a thing, but as a "you," worthy of respect and even reverence.

9. Belonging is such an important issue in well-being amid cultural plurality that Aart M. van Beek discusses it as one of three categories for pastoral assessment in intercultural care. The other two are worldview and cultural identity. Aart M. van Beek, *Cross-Cultural Counseling* (Minneapolis: Fortress Press, 1996), 59–67.

10. For more information, see www.seedsofpeace.org.

11. David Augsburger, *Pastoral Counseling across Cultures* (Philadelphia: Westminster, 1986), 27–37.

12. I develop this claim in *Reckoning with Aggression: Theology, Violence, and Vitality* (Louisville: Westminster John Knox, 1997).

13. Westerhoff, "The Birthing of the New," 59.

14. Virstan B. Y. Choy, "From Surgery to Acupuncture: An Alternative Approach to Managing Church Conflict from an Asian American Perspective," in *Conflict Management in Congregations*, ed. David B. Lott (Bethesda, Md.: Alban Institute, 2001), 141–48.

15. Emma Percy and Martyn Percy, "Strong Feelings in a Polite Church: A Re-evaluation of Anger and Aggression in Ecclesial Polity and Pastoral Praxis." Unpublished paper.

16. Arnold Mindell, *Sitting in the Fire: Large Group Transformation Using Conflict and Diversity* (Portland, Ore.: Lao Tso Press, 1995).

# CHAPTER SEVEN

# A Spiritual Journey toward Peaceful Living

## From Hospitality to Shalom

*Elizabeth Conde-Frazier*

Though we typically associate peacemaking with distant situations like the Middle East conflict or with revolutionary wars and movements in African or Latin American nations, in reality peacemaking begins with the conflict in our personal lives and communities. One such community is the congregation. As neighborhoods become more and more multicultural, so too do congregations. Often this diversity brings with it tensions and conflict.

Recently, the Partners in Urban Transformation (PUT) organization in California engaged in dialogue on such issues with pastors of multicultural congregations, denominational leaders, and scholars in theological education. The dialogue was an attempt at speaking candidly and authentically about the messiness of living into Christian community amidst the conflicts of our diversity. Because it was not a conference of experts offering quick-fix solutions, but a seminar of equals approaching the issues with the benefit of their particular practical experiences, wisdom, and skill, the participants discussed problems openly, honestly, and creatively, noting both successes and failures. With this base of practical experience, the group realized its hopes of finding solidarity in the presence of other peacemakers and gaining insights from each other for their continued work.

The dialogue especially explored the issues of power in the structure of congregations. Participants named space, time, resources, leadership style, theology, and identity as the places of power in the church. By space, the group meant how facilities were used. By time, the group was interested in how the sharing of facilities gives time or doesn't give time to each group for worship and other programs, and in how each culture understands time. The participants also related the issues of time and space to the availability of financial resources. Leadership style had to do with the image of pastor held by congregations and pastors, for example, whether he/she would function primarily as a chaplain or as an equipper and organizer. Identity referred to the issues the first-generation church had of maintaining their cultural identity and language. The ability to do this empowers the first generation, providing safety and comfort amidst the loss of ties to their country of origin.

Theological issues that the group discussed typically had a historical root to them. Often these theological differences were rooted in the missionary legacy of the last centuries, a legacy that often used — or indeed abused — theology as a way of Americanizing persons both in their countries of origin where the missionaries served and as immigrant groups to the United States. Indeed, some of the missionary literature used the terms "to evangelize" and "to Americanize" interchangeably as if there were no difference between them. Values and behavioral changes are linked to this use and abuse of theology, so that at times it led to redeemed lives, while on other occasions it led to the stripping of one's culture and thus the separation of persons from their families and cultural groups.

Cultural differences also fashion spiritual practices such as prayer and how we engage scriptures. Will we be contemplative or discursive? In some cultures prayer is a more solemn, personal moment and tends to be more contemplative. In other cultures, prayer is more communal and spontaneous, a dialogue shared by many.

In their discussions of all these aspects, the group asked how power is shaped when we speak the truth in love, and found that it often depends on styles of confrontation, respect, and voice. In some Asian cultures, for example, frontal confrontation is not the style. Confrontation is more subtle. One must read between the lines to understand that one is being confronted about something. The reason for this is that saving face is so important. I will not say something to someone that may cause them to lose face publicly. For this reason I give hints that signal to them that a change in their thoughts or behavior is warranted. In other cultures confrontation is a healthy dynamic, and it is perfectly normal to raise one's voice in the argument and to be direct with the other. To be confronted is to be respected and considered capable of changing one's understanding and behavior.

Participants in PUT also noticed how local and international issues of conflict and peace are woven together. This entanglement demands a knowledge of the pertinent history, the nature of power in different cultural settings, economic realities, and theology. Our general approach to this is social and political analysis with the hope that one can move on to strategic changes. These, however, have failed many times. Persons become discouraged before the process is finished, and the cognitive domains leave too many places to hide from the real issues at hand in the relationships. And yet, in my own experience in the church, the classroom, and community organizing I have found that relationship building is essential for going beyond cognitive constructs as a means of building peace. A spiritual journey touches the heart of the barriers that have not been transcended.

The spiritual journey I am about to explore is one that does not come out of theoretical knowledge but out of my own lived journey and that of many other pastors as well as congregations and communities that struggle every day with these issues of power across our differences. What is vital for subverting the power of hegemony is connection with others at a deep level — deep enough that it becomes incarnational relationship. This is the power that subverts all others. The spirituality that I propose that leads to peaceful coexistence embraces several spiritual disciplines: hospitality, encounter, compassion/empathy, passion, and shalom. I begin with the biblical roots of this spirituality.

## THE BIBLICAL ROOTS FOR A CHRISTIAN SPIRITUALITY FOR PEACEFUL LIVING

A Christian way of life is composed of various activities that provide concrete ways for us to flourish. A spiritual practice therefore is carried out not because it works but because it is good. It is a way of connecting God to the world around us, of connecting ourselves to our neighbors and to our environment. The outcome of the practice affects much that is beyond us. As something we do together consistently, such practices help us grow in the particular areas that we practice. We learn them in small increments of daily faithfulness. Our Christian practices of spirituality become part of our daily lives and reinforce that we are "all tangled up with the things God is doing in the world."[1] To become so entangled makes us partners in God's reconciling love for the world and, by extension, peacemakers.

One can see this entanglement with God's reconciling purposes in the New Testament and early church communities that developed in a multicultural context. Of necessity the members had to cross cultural boundaries in their practices. The incarnation and Pentecost informed the New Testament legacy on these matters: the Holy Spirit reveals Jesus Christ, God incarnate, to us. The Spirit reveals the word that became flesh and lived among us, and the Spirit summons us to continue to incarnate God in the world. What does it mean to incarnate God today? Hispanic theologian Samuel Solivan addresses the meaning of incarnation by pointing to Jesus' witness of the incarnation in the Gospel of John. "The word became flesh and lived among us, and we have seen his glory, the glory as of a father's son, full of grace and truth" (John 1:14). This verse challenges us to dwell among those who are different from ourselves. It displaces us from comfortable places and invites us instead to live within a reality that we may not have chosen for ourselves with the purpose of understanding a different context so that this understanding may move us to compassion among the peoples we have now learned to embrace. Our compassion becomes God's grace in the midst of a people who may not have understood grace otherwise or may have felt abandoned by God's grace. In this, we see "the glory as of a father's son."

Jesus' example of border crossing and his spirit of compassion inform our attitudes toward diversity. Solivan posits that the incarnation requires "that divinity take on a foreign identity as flesh...our human existence."[2] We are called to venture into the world of our neighbor, which may be both different or even strange to us and yet also very familiar. The incarnation calls us to dislocate ourselves from that which is familiar and to relocate ourselves in fellowship alongside those who are different from us. The account of the Pentecostal outpouring of the spirit of God discloses to us what God wills in the world: unity amidst diversity. "Not a suspension of difference but the free and liberating inclusion of difference mediated by the Holy Spirit in hope, love and peace."[3]

Pentecost points us toward some of our goals for becoming a multicultural community. It understands the church as a multiethnic, multilingual, and multiracial body. It instills positive attitudes toward diversity as enriching and enabling of Christian unity rather than as threatening. The Spirit enables us to value and affirm our own culture while engaging in effective ways with another culture. Pentecost also invites us to appreciate the many ways that faith is expressed in the practice of Christians from various cultures.[4] On Pentecost, the apostles and those in the upper room heard the gospel proclaimed in many different languages. Language symbolizes culture as everything we come to know in life is dressed in the names that the culture has given it. To hear the good news in different languages signals that the good news is dressed in the attire of different cultures. This was not entirely understood until the Judaic church found it necessary to wrestle with the inclusion of the Gentiles and how their expression of faith, which did not include the necessity of circumcision, brought the Jews to new theological reflections and understandings of God. As the gospel has been spread across the world, the church continues to wrestle with the relationship between the gospel message and the cultures that embrace it. Each time it is embraced, it is the Holy Spirit that leads the people in their understanding of the forms the message takes or incarnates in their context. These forms ground the gospel in that culture in relevant ways, allowing it to be woven into the fabric of their traditions.

These goals challenge both the cultural minority church as well as the cultural majority church. First, cultural minority churches need to assist their members to believe themselves to be full human beings, people with worthy experiences, histories, and aspirations. Second, cultural majority congregations need to become aware of their own cultural imperialism by making a practice of affirming the cultural heritage of each person and by teaching attitudes of respect and appreciation toward other cultures. Respect is not demonstrated by becoming blind to cultural differences; this simply renders them invisible. Instead we acknowledge the differences and participate in them. Recognition of our uniqueness and differences acknowledges the gifts that these bring to all. Discrimination does not come as a result of the recognition of differences. It is the denial of certain rights or ill treatment on the basis of those differences. In the book of Acts (16:15), when Lydia met Paul, she challenged him by saying, "If you deem me worthy come to my house." Jesus also placed himself in the position of encountering Gentile peoples (John 4:4–26; Matt. 15:21–28). This is where we need to position ourselves.

To position ourselves with those who are strangers to us allows us to hear them speak about the various dimensions of their lives from their perspective. Listening to a different perspective helps us to realize that the dimensions of our lives such as politics, education, history, and religion are indeed culturally influenced. This awareness or consciousness raising will bring us to where we will develop strong analytical skills and relational skills. It will help us to develop a more balanced approach to cultural diversity, one that combines a deep respect and understanding for one's own culture with a healthy curiosity, appreciation, valuation, and respect of persons of other cultures.[5]

## HOSPITALITY

We typically first encounter one another through acts of hospitality — or the lack of them. Hospitality, a practice of kingdom values, is a part of worshiping Jesus. Thus we are reminded in Matthew 25 that to offer food, shelter, and protection to one of these "little ones" is to offer it to Jesus. Luke 14 and the parable of inviting to the banqueting table those who cannot repay us is another image of hospitality that undergirds our practice, as it did during the fourth and fifth centuries when the church founded various institutions for the care of pilgrims and the poor. It was the monastic communities who held the demands of hospitality in tension with the ideal of separation from the world as they carried the Christian tradition of hospitality through the Middle Ages.[6]

Hospitality connects us to one another. It demands a space that is safe, personal, and comfortable. It calls for a place of respect, ac-ceptance, and friendship. It is a space where we offer each other a life-sustaining network of relations. So, for example, older immigrants offer their life-sustaining networks to newer immigrants. They may offer to translate for them a list of services that are needed during the first year along with the contact persons, market places where food from one's country may be found, childcare for the parents as they seek employment, and other necessities that make life easier during this time of adaptation to a new culture. This is a very important dimension of what the church is for first-generation persons.

When I pastored congregations in New England, I learned how im-portant it was for this place of hospitality to offer attentive listening and a mutual sharing of lives and life stories. Because persons often wished to get to know Hispanics, our congregation was invited to countless potluck dinners. Yet I found it difficult to make these events meaningful experiences because, as strangers to each other, there were many barriers between us. On one occasion, I decided to arrange for us to have an evening where we could share our lives with each other. Both communities chose four persons who would share their stories. We enjoyed a passionate, humorous, and dramatic time of storytelling. It required of us an openness of our hearts and a willingness to make our lives visible and available to each other. These initial conversations led to the idea of a Bible study where many more stories were shared in the homes of different members. Sharing our lives led persons to see connections between them. The establishment of these connections of our shared humanity was vital in later conversations in which we did not see eye to eye or where our prejudices about each other crept in. In times of conflict, engagement with each other and commitment to each other despite differences was built on these commonalities. Persons were able to challenge each other and forgive each other because the connections between them were profound and real enough to absorb the conflict.

Hospitality calls us to enlarge our hearts by offering the generosity of our time and personal resources. In our busy times, we need to remember that the Chinese characters for business are kill/heart. Our busyness takes up all of our time and we are not able to invest in kindnesses that humanize the lives of others. This may be visiting someone who is lonely, calling someone who we know needs support during a difficult time, or even inviting guests to our home to share a simple meal as a part of our Sabbath. Our busyness dictates every moment we have and curtails our ability to be hospitable.

Christine D. Pohl writes about the recovery of hospitality as a Christian tradition. She notes that because acts of hospitality participate in and reflect God's greater hospitality, they connect us to the divine, to holy ground. Hospitality is a practice of worship as well as a life-giving practice.

Hospitality is about human dignity and respect for persons, and finds its theological root in the recognition that persons have been made in the image of God. Made in that image, we were also made for others and to depend on others. This is the basic understanding for how we sympathize with the needs and suffering of others: sympathy comes because we have a common nature.

Hospitality as recognition involves respecting the image of God in another and seeing their potential contributions in a relationship as being of equal value to one's own. Valuing is of the utmost importance, for when persons are not valued they become socially invisible and their needs and concerns are not acknowledged. Therein lies the root of social injustice and suffering. Pohl rightly points out that hospitality begins a journey toward visibility.[7] It is a spiritual journey that also moves us from a practice of personal hospitality to a more broadly based practice that rearranges our social relationships.

For the two New England congregations engaged in dialogue, hospitality helped them to put aside their usual criteria of whom they associate with. This meant going beyond class and cultural differences. Professionals learned that blue-collar workers could think critically. They learned not to judge persons by their status in life. In like manner, persons who had not had the opportunity to obtain formal education learned that persons with *títulos*, or titles, after their names could have humble hearts filled with compassion.

On one occasion one of the men in the group came in late and shared with the group that his tardiness was because of the fact that one of the young people in his church had been arrested for selling drugs — which he was doing to help the family with medical expenses. The young man's mother needed pain medication for her cancer, and because he was unable to find another job, in desperation he took to selling drugs. A lawyer in the group who had been isolated because of his status immediately offered his services and even offered to employ the young man in his office. On the spot, he worked on a strategy for approaching the judge. The day's dialogue was taken up with the situation. As they left, the lawyer found others apologizing to him for having judged him wrongly. As a person with a *título* they had thought him to care only for the affairs of his personal and professional world.

In these relationships we see hospitality becoming an act of resistance. When, on the basis of our common creation and status in Christ, we practice the rearrangements of relationships through even the smallest act of respect and welcome rather than disregard and dishonor, we affirm a different system of values and an alternate model of relationships. Through this act of resistance we witness to the importance of transcending social differences and breaking with sociocultural boundaries that are exclusive. The book of James directs us to this understanding. In the second chapter, James speaks about showing preference or favoritism toward the rich and how this denial of the poor is a betrayal of the law of love. This picks up on his previous theme in the first chapter (1:26–27) where he speaks of authentic religion as one of rejecting the standards of the world (favoritism) and living instead by the standards of God by being a present help to the needy. The practice of hospitality is an embodiment of authentic religion. This practice also helps us resist the temptation of working toward social change only from a distance.

John Wesley recognized the importance of intentionally forming relationships that crossed boundaries. He noticed that when persons were in contact with their poor neighbors they could understand their neighbors' situation better and could respond more effectively as a personal practice of the ministry of love and care. Dislocating ourselves from our usual places of work, school, worship, and residence helps us break away from a dominating power and teaches us true power as Jesus exercised it: the power of self-giving and loving service to others. Such service is an expression of the church's life of holiness.

Our expressions of hospitality are to be exercised in a particular spirit or attitude of the heart, as John Chrysostom shows. He was sensitive to the fragility of the recipient of hospitality that resulted from that person's dependence on another in the act of receiving hospitality. In various homilies he exhorted his congregation to show "excessive joy" in order to avoid shaming the recipient. This stressed the importance of respect and humility in offering hospitality.[8] Such a spirit maintains the dignity of the one receiving hospitality, especially if that person is needy. This is why Romans 12:8 encourages the giver to be generous and the compassionate to be so in cheerfulness. Hospitality sprouts into compassion and, like all the other gifts, is to be exercised with the purpose of building up or edifying the body.

## ENCOUNTER

*Who knows one culture, knows no culture. We come to self-knowledge on the boundary.*[9]

Encounter is where we risk. It is a place for the collision of two worlds, for the multiplicity of views. It is where various streams meet. It is the bringing together of a variety of sources that might not often be placed together. It is at conjunctive places that we hold together what might be seen as opposite. This is the borderland. These are the spaces where hybrid significations are created that require the practice of cultural translations and negotiations. It is here that we transcend dualistic modes of thinking either/or and we come to understand how opposing ideas and knowledge can interact with and enrich each other. This place is called mestizo/a consciousness, something Gloria Anzaldúa describes as a continual walking out of one culture and into another.[10] It is the transfer of the cultural and spiritual values of one group to another. It is straddling cultures. It is a consciousness of the struggle of the border. It is hearing multiple voices at times with conflicting messages. It is what Asian theologian Jung Young Lee calls marginality or being "in-both," and it is this which restores the balance between the two poles and creates harmony.[11]

Such tolerance for ambiguity and for keeping opposites in tension is seen by James Fowler as a stage of faith. In this stage we are able to enter into cross-cultural and interfaith dialogue because we can deal with paradoxes. I believe that the Holy Spirit grants the grace for us to remain flexible enough that we can stretch the psyche horizontally and vertically that we might shift out of habitual formations. This is the gift of encounters. One way that the Holy Spirit works through these encounters is through the telling of and listening to stories.

## ENCOUNTER AS STORYTELLING AND LISTENING

In our encounters, telling and listening to stories leads us to deeper relationship. To share the stories of our daily pain and hope is to make new meaning which results in deeper ethnic and Christian identities. This movement of storytelling is where we first recognize that those in the dominant culture have constructed the church to fit their needs; it is their voice that has been heard from the pulpits, theological classrooms, theological books, and denominational hierarchies. Now it is time for others to be heard as well. Encounter is the place for shared experience. This means letting the silenced stories be heard, even before our own. It begins with the act of appreciation of our neighbor.

These encounters are experiences. An experience is what happens to a person. It is what we feel, see, and live through. It is the actions and events of our lives. In this case, it is the continuum of encounters that we share with the neighbor. Our continuums of experiences are usually woven into stories. Educators Clandinin and Connelly claim that family stories about the world are usually told in such a way that younger generations listening will understand the world through the experiences of the elders.[12] In immigrant communities, this intergenerational storytelling is sometimes reversed, with the younger and not the older generation doing the telling — because they're doing the experiencing — about the ways of a new world. In this manner, the stories also help to forge community identity. To tell the stories of our encounters is a way of teaching new attitudes to the next generation. We can, if we choose, break with the legacy of prejudices in our present story or relationship with one another. This would be reflected in stories where the usually marginalized person now becomes someone like us with similar fears, hopes, faults, and gifts. It can be told as a story where the once other is now a person with whom we share and are familiar. This shifts the paradigm of relationship. This shift illustrates a transformation of perspective and is important for changing our attitudes and behaviors.

In our stories we find what James Loder defines as transforming moments or moments of faith transformation.[13] For Loder, these moments alter our ways of being in the world. A transforming moment is a convictional experience. It disrupts our assumptive world by puncturing our previous ways of making meaning, and it discloses to us dimensions of being not previously attended to, which enables us to reground and realign our ways of seeing and being. These are the moments that are apparent in our stories.

Listening is an accompanying movement to telling the story. Pastor Brian Parcel, whose church is in a changing neighborhood, led his Anglo congregation through a process of listening to the stories of their Latino neighbors at a cookout that the church offered its neighbors in a nearby park. He encourages us

> to listen to our soul where lies the common place we all share with one another. Somewhere deep within our soul underneath the layers of power, dominance and difference that we hear and see in this world, there is the common place — our humanity. If we listen from this place we can get beyond the impulses to protect ourselves from what we hear, to reject what we hear and to judge what we hear and then we can just listen to the story of the other person.[14]

The women of Rev. Parcel's congregation found that as widows they had much in common with the single mothers in their neighborhood. It helped them to see their neighbors as friends rather than unapproachable strangers. Seeing others as strangers can keep us from opening up to the possibilities of creative ministries with our neighbors.

Such an encounter begins at the surface. We approach with faith, our initial way of seeing and understanding. We know that there is something more than what we now see. We have a sense that what we see we cannot fully understand. We do not have the proper tools for interpreting what we see. If we tried, we would only project our own reality upon what we see. It is better to wait. It is at this stage of the process of understanding that a church congregation may walk through its changing neighborhood in order to observe the new sounds, smells, and colors, even though it may not yet know what they point to. We can observe but we cannot decode. We cannot make connections between the lived phrases of people's lives, and a reading is impossible to us.

At this phase of the interaction Parcel encourages us to listen to the stories told in demographic information without necessarily looking for a quick solution but letting the dissonance be played on the strings of our hearts where our compassion and passion may emerge. We must listen to what our congregation's stories tell of inward- or outward-focused ministries. We must listen to the stories of the voting district's monthly meeting or the PTA meetings. What stories do they tell? Who is in need? Who is crying out? Who has gifts to offer? Who is not listened to? What common ground do we see?

A Latino congregation in New York City was facing the reality of its neighborhood changing to a lower-income neighborhood with all of its celebrations and problems. After almost fifty years there they did not know the dynamics of the lives of their neighbors, and therefore they were unable to proclaim the gospel in ways that made it relevant to their problems, needs, and routines of daily life. They started to visit with their neighbors every Tuesday night during the summer instead of holding a midweek worship service. They carefully noted the recurring themes of their stories, which the church members later wove in with the biblical story. The conversations also yielded relationships with their neighbors that became instrumental for combining the leadership of the church and the community for working on projects and eventually community organizing together.

The sharing of stories was crucial for getting to this point of partnership in the community. How can we communicate stories when language might be a barrier? Stories can be told through art, music, dance, and drama in order to transcend language barriers. They break down the master narrative of our society, and the master paradigms begin to shift. This shifting of the master paradigms may entail telling the difficult parts of our common history. Relaying the stories of discrimination and racism is difficult, but if we are to rearrange relationships then we must deconstruct how the common story was put together. This is what has taken place in South Africa as victims have told their stories in the presence of their victimizers. The common story of their brokenness is being told, permitting both victims and victimizers to imagine the possibilities of a different story passing between them.

An example of this can be seen in what took place in San Diego in 2003, when there was an exhibit of portraits and stories of participants in a national forum called the Arab-Jewish Dialogues. The forum brings together about 150 persons in six chapters who meet once a month to talk about their differences and their common fears. Jews and Arabs get to know each other and their long-held prejudices. Participants have confessed that they have learned to stop dehumanizing one another and have come to respect one another. Becoming familiar with one another's personal narratives has been key to this process.[15]

When the unspeakable is spoken, it can no longer be denied. Denial is wounding for us. It leads to the cesspools of guilt and unresolved anger. To convert knowledge to acknowledgment involves confession as well as giving support to the victim so that justice can flow.

The Christian story enacted also helps us change our master narratives. Pohl speaks of a person who participated in the *posadas*, a Hispanic Christmas tradition that enacts the story of Mary and Joseph

going from door to door requesting shelter, and being turned away repeatedly before finding a place where Jesus can be born. As the man
in question experienced the story in this way, he connected with the
experience of being homeless and of becoming aware of God's presence
in homeless persons.

Within our encounters, whether ritualized like in the *posadas* or in
our everyday neighborhood activities, the Holy Spirit helps to birth
new stories. Such was the case when Peter visited Cornelius (Acts 10).
The vision Peter received of the large sheet coming down with all kinds
of four-footed creatures — reptiles and birds of the air, including those
the law prohibited him to eat — expanded the realm of the possible for
him. The journey began for him with great puzzlement (Acts 10:17).
As Peter went to Cornelius's home and shared freely in the hospitality
offered at his Gentile neighbor's home, the Holy Spirit opened him up
to new experiences and life directions. Peter preached, and while he
was still speaking the Holy Spirit fell upon all who heard the word.
Again, astonishment filled Peter and the circumcised believers with
him at seeing the Holy Spirit poured out "even on the Gentiles" (Acts
10:45) who were not circumcised. The Holy Spirit had taken them
beyond the cultural and religious interpretations that had alienated
Jews and Gentiles from one another. Later, Paul is able to reinterpret
these events into a new Christian story that includes both Jews and
Gentiles in a new relationship.

> He has abolished the law with its commandments and ordinances,
> that he might create in himself one new humanity in place of the
> two, thus making peace, and might reconcile both groups to God
> in one body through the cross, thus putting to death that hostility
> through it.... So then you are no longer strangers and aliens but
> you are ... members of the household of God. (Eph. 2:13–16, 19)

I wonder what new stories the Holy Spirit is birthing today as we visit
with our neighbors across cultures, across traditional gender definitions,

and even across religious experiences? What new directions and possibilities is the Spirit opening up to us? We know from looking at the stories that the Holy Spirit initiates that they are narratives of reconciliation. These narratives go beyond the cultural and religious barriers that keep us as strangers and aliens to one another.

What do we listen for in the stories? We are listening for God's revelation, symbols and commonalities between our worlds that may point to common wounds and passions for the world, the call of God in our lives to the world, and self-awareness.

## COMPASSION

The word "compassion" is derived from the words *cum* and *patior*, which mean to suffer with, to undergo with. It connotes solidarity. Compassion therefore works from a place of strength through mutuality. It is participating in the sufferings of another from a strength born of awareness of shared weakness.[16] It is this sense of shared weakness that distinguishes compassion from pity. Pity takes more distance from the one suffering and sees him/her as weak or inferior. In pity, there is less participation in the suffering of the other person.

Compassion and joy are linked. In Romans 12:8, the grace of the gift of compassion is cheerfulness. In compassion as well as in celebration, it is the togetherness that is empowering. We share our sufferings and our joys — passion with. Matthew Fox points out that celebration and compassion are a forgetting in order to remember. We forget or let go of ego and concerns in order to remember the common base that makes another's suffering mine. Then together we can imagine a relief or solution for that suffering.[17] In celebration we also let go of ego and concerns in order to share in the joy of a relief brought about.

Compassion involves imagination and action. The story of the Good Samaritan speaks of the Samaritan's works of mercy. These works make it clear that compassion is not about sentimentalism. Anne Douglas denies sentimentalism as "the political sense obfuscated or gone rancid . . . (that) never exists except in tandem with failed political consciousness."[18] Works of mercy are described by the prophets (Isa. 58:6–7; Mic. 6:6–8) and in the Johannine literature where we are exhorted to love in truth and action (1 John 3:18). This action is described as a laying down of one's life for one another and helping those in need (1 John 3:16–17). The book of James creates a dialectic between faith and works (James 2:14–22), inviting us to be both hearers and doers of the word (James 1:22). In the Gospels Jesus shows us what the works of mercy look like in his stories. In the acts of the healings and miracles, we see Jesus moved to compassion. The power for healing and doing miracles is the power of compassion.

An expression of compassion can be seen in the following account. In the Latino community a great number of us lack health insurance. Health care is a luxury so that prayers for healing are common. One of the names ascribed to Jesus in our community is "the most excellent doctor" (*el médico por excelencia*). Healing services are not the drama portrayed by televangelists but the prayers of the compassionate poor pooling their faith on behalf of a beloved one suffering in the community that relief might come. In one such community, a man in a wheelchair sat in the front at every service of his storefront congregation. One evening, the invited preacher was overwhelmed by weeping during the sermon so that he could not finish it. Instead, he moved with compassion toward the wheelchair and uttered a humble whispered prayer for the man who was sitting in it. The congregation prayed with him although his words could not be heard. At the end of the prayer a closing hymn was sung, during which the man in the wheelchair stood up and danced with tears of joy.

On other occasions, compassion takes the form of doing justice. Marcion wrote of a dualism between the good God and the just God, creating a polarity between mercy and justice.[19] This separated justice and love. In the United States, before the civil rights movement and at many other moments, churches have spoken of love but have not been able to articulate what that love looked like. During the movement,

Dr. Martin Luther King Jr. equated justice with love. He said, "Justice is love correcting that which would work against love."[20] Before this statement and the actions of the civil rights movement, the relationship between theology and politics in the active life of the church was bifurcated. There were few who claimed that the two could mix successfully, and so they chose silence instead. Others advocated a form of gradualism which naturally denounced more radical expressions such as sit-ins and boycotts. These political, nonviolent strategies were the works of mercy or compassion. In this religious and theological context, Martin Luther King Jr. and other church people began to relate the Christian gospel to the struggle for justice in the United States. They named desegregation as the expression or action of that love. As King's own understanding of justice grew, he linked justice with the need to alleviate poverty for all citizens and later with the need for peace in the world, naming militarism an evil. When compassion's link with justice is made clear to us, so too is its expression of anger. Anger has not generally been considered a positive emotion.[21] Like conflict, it has traditionally been considered a spiritual impediment. Yet, anger in Spanish is *coraje*, which also means courage, and Aristotle defined anger as an energy that enables us to face difficulty. Thomas Aquinas integrated Aristotle's view into Christian thinking to give us an expanded and more positive view of anger. Anger is a gift from God and also an emotion that God displays. As Kathleen Greider writes in her chapter, it brings out resistance rather than helplessness. A person with a healthy sense of self who is hurt in any way will be aroused to protest. This expression of protest is anger. It is a necessary part of our survival. Yet beyond survival, anger also serves social transformation.[22] As prophets today, we must combine our anger with the spiritual discipline of temperance so that it can be cooled to a productive level and bear the spiritual fruits of justice (love), hope, and peace.[23]

Perhaps the concept of *hesed* can help nurture the discipline of temperance and channel the energy of our anger for social transformation. *Hesed* is the Hebrew word that is translated as compassion or mercy.

Scholars agree that there is no one word that can adequately translate *hesed* into English. *Hesed* is something that one does with someone. It implies the doing of deliverance that justice is about.[24] Many times this doing of justice becomes a cause and we lose sight of persons. Causes require heroes and heroines, leaders who stand in the spotlight. This tendency corrupts the spirit of doing justice. On the other hand, *hesed* or compassion is moving out of our egocentricity. Egocentricity is a state of ego-defense. It is the very stuff of which prejudices are made. Compassion is transcendence of the self. This transcendence is reflected in the first epistle of John, "No one has ever seen God; if we love one another, God lives in us" (1 John 4:12) and also, "everyone who loves is born of God and knows God, for God is love" (1 John 4:8).

Compassion, as part of the journey of conversion, brings us from indifference to care. It also helps us redefine our inner parameters so that we go from giving precedence to blood ties or ties to family and culture to embracing the needs of the whole created family. Compassion is the internalizing of others to where we no longer feel displaced or dislocated when interacting outside of our culture. Instead, our sense of what joins us to those who had previously been strangers is a common humanity, a new understanding of who we are and who others are to us. It comes from a knowledge of the *corazón,* or heart, the "biological symbolic site of wisdom and knowledge. It is a metaphor for the whole of one's conscious, intelligent and free personality. The heart integrates and informs aspects of a person including the mind, will and emotions. This is close to the biblical understanding of heart which refers to the core and center of a person and the source of ultimate understanding."[25] Therefore, compassion is the process whereby we connect to others, allowing them to pervade us until they become significant in our lives.

As these connections take place we learn empathy. Empathy makes us aware of the world of our neighbor in the way that our neighbor experiences it. Heinz Kohut of South Africa says of empathy that it is the essential ingredient for human life. Through empathy we mirror or validate and confirm the experience of the other person, and in turn our experiences are also validated. Empathy permits us to step back from our own feelings while not disavowing them, to put ourselves in the place of the other person, by vicariously grasping that person's emotional experience.[26] When we have compassion we are able to listen empathetically and to confront or contradict misinformation or injustice because we are seeking the well-being of the neighbor based on our capacity to grasp their experience. In light of this, our understanding of relationships and power is challenged.

The two congregations in New England found such a place of compassion when it came to the education of their children. The Anglo congregation was shocked at the poor quality of education received by the children of their Latino brothers and sisters. This discovery led first to anger and then to analysis of why this was so. The Anglo members were shocked a second time to discover that the system worked differently for different persons. Their compassion led them together in two directions: the first was to set up an after-school tutoring program; the second was collecting signatures for a petition for more funds in the budget for the school district where the church was located. The bonds formed during these years served to cement the two congregations and others in the community for work on other problems as well.

It is from this new understanding of the relationship between self and neighbor that true compassion can be birthed. It is a perspective that comes through the lens of humility. Humility has a balanced understanding of self-worth. It is not self-debasement but self-acceptance. It does not see itself as greater than another and therefore does not usurp the place of another. This sense of self and neighbor allows us to relate to one another not according to the social and economic status of our cultures but according to our true human worth. Compassion needs to allow for equal partnership or it may be expressed in ways that create dependency or false love. Pity, for example, perceives others as unable to do for themselves and the self as the one who has the power to bring change to the unfortunate circumstances of others' lives. It is birthed from a hidden sense of pride. Compassion, however, does not strip others of their dignity and power to act on their own behalf but partners with them, complementing their gifts and efforts toward humanization.

## PASSION

Compassion is passionate. The compassionate God is a passionate God. Compassion is about being moved. It is a movement.[27] Because we have, in some way, entered into the pain of our neighbor, shared it and tasted it in so far as that is possible, then we are moved. So, just as deep calls unto deep, compassion invites passion. After listening to each other's stories and getting to know our diverse gifts, we are connected by a common wound in the place where our two worlds have encountered each other. Passion is derived from the Latin word *patior*, meaning to suffer or to take on. To stand with Jesus is to share his passion.

Jesus' passion can be seen in the incarnation event as well as the announcement of the reign of God through the actions of Jesus' ministry. When Jesus erupts into our history he announces that the time has been fulfilled and God's reign is at hand (Mark 1:9–14). The National Conference of Catholic Bishops, in their pastoral letter on social teachings, sees this proclamation as a "summons to acknowledge God as creator and covenant partner."[28] This can only be done when our commitment to God is enacted through love of one's neighbor. This enactment of the word is the truth taking form in us. That form is devotion. Devotion is the act or condition of giving oneself up for another person, purpose, or service. It is setting ourselves apart for this type of deep, steady affection as our spiritual worship. It entails the grasping of that which is not normally accessible, the apprehending of the invisible God and the people visible to God but made invisible by injustices. To reveal these injustices is to reveal those who live under their weight and to see the invisible God visible through them. Devotion is a sacred and reverent expression of the totality of our person. The fruit of such worship is solidarity.[29]

This devotion is what characterizes our priesthood. The priesthood is the privilege of being broken. It is the privilege of the cross. It is the privileges of losses, grief, and tears, but we remember that Jesus also wept. It was his compassion that caused the power of healing and of resurrection to be released on behalf of others. In his book *Who Comes in the Name of the Lord?* Harold Recinos reminds us that the cup symbolizes Jesus' suffering witness before the powerful. Drinking from it implies entering into radical solidarity with the way — and the One — of the cross.[30]

This radical solidarity can be seen in the work of a congregation that works with persons at the border. They provide sanctuary, helping persons cross from the U.S. border into Canada.[31] The bodies of these refugees showed the torture they had experienced in their countries. However, because of the United States' support of the political leaders in power in those countries and because of our own complicity in the terror in those countries, political asylum had been denied to many who could not return home. To become involved in such a ministry places us outside the law. If we were caught, it would mean incarceration. Much soul searching and prayer was a part of the discernment process. The congregation understood that this was the way of the cross and part of their call to the priesthood of all believers. They looked to the cloud of witnesses in their past who had been part of the abolitionist movement and had participated in the Underground Railroad that brought enslaved persons from the South to the free northern states. Passion provided strength to respond to this call.

The empathy stirs our souls, and in this stirring the spirit impassions us. The passion comes from reflection upon and participation in the divine pathos where God is involved in the life of the community. Passion is intimacy and sympathy with God and with humanity. It is divine consciousness and neighbor consciousness engaging each other. This borderland existence enables us to be soaked in God's tears that locate places in need of the spirit's gift of wholeness, faith, hope, and love. This empowers us to bring life-giving fruits and wisdom to the struggles of our communities. It is a loving entering into the world of the neighbor. This caring disposition moves us to interact with and on behalf of those we love. It is a common pathos and passion that now unites us. Those things that break our hearts and make us angry and which we therefore wish to change are the things that we now hold in common.

Passion asks, what is the nature of suffering? What is faith? What does it mean to "walk humbly with God"?[32] What would it be like to lead a life that is whole and integrated? Passion is seeking for and finding meaning in life. It invites us to commitment to relationship and community. Passion is the making of a disciple. It involves the integration of knowledge with values and vocation precisely because it is grounded in relationship with others. Passion is the courage to take risks in order to pursue what one believes gives life meaning. Through it, we become people who have vibrant spiritual lives.

When our love for those who suffer and the love of the heart of God for those who are in need of justice come together in us, our hearts become a borderland between God and humanity — a prophetic space. Our initial connection with one another has now matured and facilitates the building of shalom together.

## SHALOM

This section is the shortest of all. The reason is that it seeks to catch glimpses of a vision that I have not yet seen fully realized. It is a vision of reconciliation that involves not only congregations and the communities they are located in but also the systems that interlock with one another the world over. It is a vision still under construction that we grasp with the eyes of our faith.

Shalom is a concept that cannot be captured by a single English word, for it includes many dimensions: love, loyalty, truth, grace, salvation, justice, blessing, and righteousness. It is a biblical vision of world history where all of creation is one, every creature in community with every other, living in harmony and security toward the joy and well-being of every other creature. Shalom is therefore a vision of connectedness by and for a whole community: young, elderly, rich, poor, Latino, Anglo, Native American, Asian, African American, gay and straight, powerful and dependent. Shalom includes the process of denouncing, announcing, and making persons and structures responsible for responding equitably and compassionately to all.

Finally, shalom is not shifting the center of power from one center to another, but it is distributing power among all equally. Because equity or reconciliation is our final goal, we cannot hold metaphors or visions of the center. Asian theologian Jung Young Lee proposes a multicultural theology in which marginality is that which overcomes our need for centrality. He reminds us that centrality is based on hierarchical value, is interested in dominance, and vies for control, while marginality is based on an egalitarian principle, is interested in service, and seeks cooperation.[33] Lee invites us all to the margin rather than to the center. He posits that when everyone becomes marginal, there is no centrality that can marginalize anyone so that marginality is overcome by marginality.[34]

Latino theologian Orlando Costas also invites us to the margins as he reminds us that Christ died outside the gate, which implies a new place of salvation. The temple had been the central place of salvation, a place confined to the walls of the city, but Jesus died outside, at the margins. He displaced salvation from the center to the margins.[35]

The journey from hospitality to shalom is one of the spiritual practices that frees us from the inclination to dominate and control and instead teaches us to be servants to all people so that all are served as brothers and sisters equally. It is this spirit that makes us a people guided by the spirit of the incarnation.

## CONCLUSION

While Moses was living in the desert there was a whole people living enslaved in Egypt. When God revealed their reality to Moses, then Moses included their world in his world. Through hearing their story, the faceless "others" whom he did not know were revealed to him. This revelation or encounter brought him to the discovery of the connections between the everyday life of his neighbor (their life of slavery) and his own life. Now, the historical events of his time, which had had no meaning for him, entered into his world with new meaning. Moses now had pangs of conscience.

Now, the way that Moses understood the meaning of life changed. The stranger, the "other," became his neighbor. Furthermore, Moses was to come to the understanding of this God through the liberation of the people in bondage. This is the love that leads to justice. If Moses did not go out to liberate this people, he would be conscious of having committed sin.[36]

God's revelation is found in God's revealing to Moses the people invisible to Moses but visible to God. To open himself to them is to open himself to God. To shut out the slave is to shut God out. Storytelling then is a medium for the revelation of God. Moses' life was changed upon appropriating the story of the slaves not as an event or a memory but as a moment of conversion where he now internalized God by internalizing the slaves in Egypt. Moses, God, and the enslaved peoples became intertwined in a story of liberation.

Can this spiritual journey lead us toward worldwide fellowship in which the life of an African American, a Vietnamese, a Latina, a gay brother or a lesbian sister, an Afghani, a North Korean, an Iraqi is as precious as my own life? This is a journey toward a vision of the spiritual values of compassion, generosity, and community. These values make solidarity and shalom materialize among us. May they lead us into new stories of peacemaking that reveal God in our midst.

## NOTES

1. Craig Dykstra and Dorothy Bass, "Times of Yearning, Practices of Faith," in *Practicing Our Faith*, ed. Dorothy C. Bass (San Francisco: Jossey-Bass, 1997), 8.

2. Samuel Solivan, "The Holy Spirit-Personalization and the Affirmation of Diversity: A Pentecostal Hispanic Perspective," in *Teología en Conjunto: A Collaborative Hispanic Protestant Theology*, ed. José David Rodríguez and Loida I. Martell-Otero (Louisville: Westminster John Knox, 1997), 59.

3. Ibid., 60.

4. Adapted from the original goals in "Goals of Multicultural Religious Education," in *Multicultural Religious Education*, ed. Barbara Wilkerson (Birmingham, Ala.: Religious Education Press, 1997), 26–27.

5. See Kathy Black, *Culturally Conscious Worship* (St. Louis: Chalice Press, 2000).

6. Christine D. Pohl, *Making Room: Recovering Hospitality as a Christian Tradition* (Grand Rapids: Eerdmans, 1999), 6.

7. Ibid., 62.

8. John Chrysostom, Homily 45 on Acts, quoted in Pohl, *Making Room*, 269.

9. David W. Augsburger, *Conflict and Mediation across Cultures: Pathways and Patterns* (Louisville: Westminster/John Knox, 1992), 9.

10. Gloria Anzaldúa, *Borderlands/La Frontera: The New Mestizo* (San Francisco: Aunt Lute Books, 1999), 99.

11. Jung Young Lee, *Marginality: The Key to Multicultural Theology* (Minneapolis: Fortress Press, 1995), chapter 2.

12. D. Jean Clandinin and F. Michael Connelly, *Narrative Inquiry: Experience and Story in Qualitative Research* (San Francisco: Jossey-Bass, 2000), 113.

13. See James E. Loder, *The Transforming Moment: Understanding Convictional Experiences* (San Francisco: Harper & Row, 1981).

14. Brian Parcel, "A Multicultural Model for Religious Education," in *Multicultural Models for Religious Education*, ed. Elizabeth Conde-Frazier (Atlanta: SCP/Third World Literature Publishing House, 2001), 40–41.

15. Janet Saidi, "Art Shows Arabs, Jews Reaching Out," *Los Angeles Times*, February 2, 2003, B6.

16. Matthew Fox, *A Spirituality Named Compassion and the Healing of the Global Village, Humpty Dumpty and Us* (Minneapolis: Winston Press, 1979), 2.

17. Ibid., 4.

18. Anne Douglas, *The Feminization of American Culture* (New York: Knopf, 1977), 54, as quoted in Fox, *A Spirituality Named Compassion*, 5.

19. For further discussion, see Hans Jonas, *The Gnostic Religion* (Boston: Beacon Press, 1963).

20. Martin Luther King Jr., "Address to the Initial Mass Meeting of the Montgomery Improvement Association," at the Holt Street Baptist Church on December 5, 1955. The tape and printed copy of this address are located in the Martin Luther King Jr. Papers, Center for Non-Violent Social Change, Atlanta.

21. The following passage is taken from Elizabeth Conde-Frazier, "Hispanic Protestant Spirituality," in Rodríguez and Martell-Otero, eds., *Teología en Conjunto,* 143.

22. James D. Whitehead and Evelyn Eaton Whitehead, *Shadows of the Heart: A Spirituality of the Negative Emotions* (New York: Crossroad, 1994), 46.

23. Ibid., 47.

24. Fox, *A Spirituality Named Compassion,* 11.

25. Daniel G. Groody, *Border of Death, Valley of Life: An Immigrant Journey of Heart and Spirit* (Lanham, Md.: Rowman & Littlefield, 2002), 8.

26. Leonard M. Hummel, "Heinz Kohut and Empathy: A Perspective from a Theology of the Cross," *Word and World: Theology for Christian Ministry* (Winter 2001): 64–74.

27. Fox, *A Spirituality Named Compassion,* 20.

28. National Conference of Catholic Bishops, *Economic Justice for All: Pastoral Letter on Catholic Social Teaching and the United States Economy* (Washington, D.C.: United States Catholic Conference, 1986), 41.

29. "Solidarity" is a term derived from the Latin *solidare,* which means to join together firmly. Michael A. Kelly traces the origin of the term. He shows how it was shaped by the changes brought about by the Enlightenment and the Industrial and French Revolutions. While the deconstruction of the old regimes brought a popular spirit of freedom, a vision was needed to carry out the systemic realization of equality. The French and the Germans made significant contributions to the exploration of such a vision and, in so doing, gave shape to the theme of solidarity. Each attempt at the vision sought to give shape to a global basis of the common good or to the Christian idea of love realized in the sociopolitical sphere, where people would live for others in the service of all humanity. Philosophical, sociological, and religious expressions were explored in this endeavor. For further discussion, see Michael A. Kelly, "Solidarity: A Foundational Educational Concern," *Religious Education* 93 (Winter 1998): 44–64.

30. Harold J. Recinos, *Who Comes in the Name of the Lord? Jesus at the Margins* (Nashville: Abingdon, 1997), 71.

31. I cannot give away the name or the location of this congregation because its work would be placed at risk.

32. Keith Morton, "Making Meaning: Reflections on Community Service and Learning," in *From Cloister to Commons: Concepts and Models for Service Learning in Religious Studies,* ed. Richard Devine, Joseph A. Farazza, and F. Michael McLain (Washington, D.C.: American Association for Higher Education, 2002), 45.

33. Lee, *Marginality,* 151.

34. Ibid.

35. See Orlando E. Costas, *Christ Outside the Gate: Mission beyond Christendom* (Grand Rapids: Eerdmans, 1986).

36. Enrique Dussel, *History and the Theology of Liberation* (Maryknoll, N.Y.: Orbis Books, 1976), 6–7.

# CONTRIBUTORS

**Philip A. Amerson** is the President of the Claremont School of Theology and a Professor of Church and Society. His academic specialty is Sociology of Religion. He has extensive work experience as a United Methodist pastor and researcher in the area of urban ministry, racism, and peacebuilding. He has taught in a number of graduate school settings and was a consultant on Urban Congregational Life for the Lilly Endowment. He is author of numerous publications and serves on a wide-ranging set of ecumenical and denominational boards and commissions.

**Elizabeth Conde-Frazier** is an Associate Professor of Religious Education at Claremont who integrates the discipline of religious education with theology, spirituality, and the social sciences. She has written on multicultural issues, Hispanic theological education, and the spirituality of the scholar. She also teaches at the Latin American Bible Institute in La Puente and has taught in Kazakhstan. Her scholarly passions involve her in participatory action research with communities working on justice issues. She seeks to do collaborative research and teaching in the areas of immigration and ecumenism as these relate to religious education. She is an ordained American Baptist minister with more than ten years' experience in the local church.

**Andrew Dreitcer** is the Director of Spiritual Formation and Associate Professor of Spirituality at Claremont. He has been a Presbyterian pastor, seminary instructor, director of seminary programs in spiritual formation and spiritual direction, retreat leader, and spiritual director. His interests include the role of scripture in spiritual life, congregational spiritual formation, and spiritual formation in theological studies. Dr. Dreitcer's spiritual life was significantly shaped by a year spent in the French community of Taizé. His recent coauthored book is entitled *Beyond the Ordinary: Spirituality for Church Leaders* (Eerdmans).

**Kathleen J. Greider** is Professor of Pastoral Care and Counseling at Claremont. Her scholarly interests are in the interrelationship of personality and culture. Her teaching, research, and writing are in the areas of pastoral theology, care and counseling, psychology and religion, and feminist and cultural analysis. Ordained by the United Methodist Church, she has clinical pastoral experience in the practice of parish ministry, pastoral psychotherapy, spiritual direction, in-patient mental health, and hospital chaplaincy. In addition to articles and essays, she is the author of *Reckoning with Aggression: Theology, Violence, and Vitality* (Westminster John Knox, 1997).

**Carol Lakey Hess** is Associate Professor of Religious Education at Claremont. She is very interested in issues dealing with feminist pedagogy and diversity in the classroom, and she plans to do more writing around this issue in the future. She is author of *Caretakers of our Common House: Women's Development in Communities of Faith*. Her newest interest is in fiction and theology, and she is currently working on a book tentatively titled *Fiction as Soul Truth: The Use of Fiction in Theology and Religious Formation*. She is also an ordained PCUSA minister.

**Ellen Ott Marshall** is an Associate Professor of Ethics at Claremont. She focuses on contemporary Christian ethics. She is particularly interested in issues of violence and peacemaking, ethical questions in literature and film, the virtue of hope in the Christian tradition, and the dynamic relationship between faith, history, and ethics. She has published essays on welfare reform and the use of film to teach ethics.

Dr. Marshall has also worked with the refugee resettlement programs of Church World Service and the United Methodist Committee on Relief.

**Frank Rogers Jr.** is the Director of Narrative Pedagogies Project and Adjunct Professor of Religious Education at Claremont. His research focus is on the use of the narrative arts (storytelling, drama, creative writing) for religious education, spiritual formation, and communal empowerment. He has worked in a variety of contexts — parishes, schools, camps, and community centers. His interests also include spiritual formation, justice education, and care for abused and marginalized young people. He has written several articles on spirituality and education and is currently completing his first novel.

**John W. Woell** is Assistant Professor of Philosophy and Religion at Greensboro College in Greensboro, North Carolina. He is currently working on a manuscript on the relationship between contemporary analytic philosophy and classical American pragmatism and pursuing research on the relationships among epistemology, ethical argumentation, and democratic deliberation. He also teaches in theology, moral and political philosophy, philosophy of religion, and aesthetics.

# INDEX OF SCRIPTURAL REFERENCES

# GENERAL INDEX